OUT OF THE SHADOWS

The Legacy of Two Holocaust Survivors

Piri Piroska Bodnar

Edited by
Marsha C. Markman, Ph.D.

authorHOUSE™

1663 LIBERTY DRIVE, SUITE 200
BLOOMINGTON, INDIANA 47403
(800) 839-8640
WWW.AUTHORHOUSE.COM

First published by AuthorHouse 3/13/2006

Revised Edition

ISBN: 1-4208-5803-3 (sc)

Printed in the United States of America
Bloomington, Indiana

This book is printed on acid-free paper.

Library of Congress Control Number: 2005904881

Piri Piroska Mendelovitz Bodnar, DOB 1925

Zoltan Bodnar, DOB 1925

*Dedicated with everlasting love to our dear children,
Kitty and Eric, for the immense joy and sunshine
they bring to our lives. Their kindness and compassion toward
their fellow human beings have always made us proud.*

*And to people around the globe who suffer from the effects of
prejudice and discrimination because of the color of
their skin, their religious beliefs, their ethnicity, or their
nationality. It would be a better world if we judged people by
their kindness, compassion, and morality.*

*In loving memory of the six million Jewish martyrs of the
Nazi Holocaust and the righteous Gentiles who risked their
lives to save thousands of Jews from certain death.*

**We can never forget
The world must never forget**

Acknowledgements

My sincere appreciation to California Lutheran University for making me part of the college community these many years.

To Dr. Marsha Markman, mentor and dear friend, for her inspiration, emotional support, the innumerable hours she spent listening to our experiences, and for her writing advice and editing. Without her this book would not have been written.

Heartfelt thanks to Dr. Ted LaBrenz for his patient editing of my early writing and the first draft of *Shadows* ("Piri's Story"). Many thanks to Dr. Janice Bowman, who read both manuscripts; Dr. Jack Ledbetter who read my poetry; Dana [Donely] Cordero for her considerable work on *Shadows*, and Drs. Robert Meadows, Pamela Jolicoeur, Michael Doyle, Sigmar Schwarz, Joel Edwards, Joseph Everson, Gerry Swanson, Jerry Miller, Luther Luedtke and Jerry Caplan who encouraged me along the way.

Special thanks to our dear son-in-law, Don Plank, who has brought so much pleasure into our lives; to Heather Teoh and Katherine Boyd who typed and proofread Zoli's manuscript; and to my special friend, Mark Markman.

And to my beloved sister, Shari, who, throughout our trials, encouraged me to be strong. Without her I would not have survived.

Piri Piroska Bodnar

Introduction

I met Piri Piroska Bodnar in the spring of 1991 when she was auditing a class at California Lutheran University. Piri's professor told her that I was teaching a course on "The Holocaust in Literature and Film" and introduced us, launching a long and close friendship. Piri told me that she is a Holocaust survivor who, in 1944 with the Nazi occupation of Hungary, was forced from her home to a ghetto and thereafter to Auschwitz and forced labor camps.

Each time we met during that semester she elaborated upon her experiences: the loss of all but three members of her once-large family; incidents she witnessed and suffered in the camps; and her husband, Zoli's ordeal. "Even during the worst of times," Piri told me, "I had faith and trust in God," a faith she learned from her grandfather who provided the inspiration that sustained her then and comforts her now. "I thank God," she said, "for every minute that I'm alive because of the many people who did not survive."

In those early discussions, Piri showed me some of her poetry and the beginnings of a memoir she was writing. Dr. Ted LaBrenz was the first of many of us on the faculty who read her notes and encouraged her to continue writing. (*Shadows*, was published in 1998 and is included and edited as "Piri's Story" in this volume.) With the publication of *Out of the Shadows*, both Piri's and Zoli's memoirs, Piri has achieved her primary goal: to leave a legacy for her children, Kitty and Eric. Equally important is her wish to see that young people learn about this tragic period in history from the "voice" of a survivor.

It was toward the end of that first semester that I asked Piri if she would like to speak to my class. She had never spoken publicly, she said, and was concerned that her Hungarian-accented English and an occasional search for English words to express herself would make it difficult for students to understand her. Her Holocaust experiences, she added, continued to cause her anxiety, all of which amounted to a daunting task. While I assured her that other survivors shared her experience and apprehension, I didn't want to add to her suffering.

Before I could rescind my invitation, however, Piri said, with sudden determination, "I will speak!" She quickly added that she must talk about the Holocaust, as must all survivors. "All too soon," she said, "none of us will be left to bear witness." She would tell the students about her childhood in Hungary, her experiences under Nazi persecution, and she would answer their questions. However, she would do so only if I sat beside her, which I did then and did so, at her insistence, across the years. One last request was that she would speak to the students when they had sufficient knowledge about the Holocaust to prepare questions for her.

So it was that, by the time Piri spoke to the class in the final few weeks of the semester the students, who represented nearly every major in the University's curriculum, had as much information about the Holocaust as could be crammed into the previous three months. There were lectures, class discussions, documentary films, a wide range of historical material, literature in a variety of genres, and a weekly dialogue journal between each student and me. Throughout the years guest speakers included other survivors, the child of survivors and a retired Army colonel whose unit liberated two concentration camps.

I told Piri about the projects the students were submitting and reporting orally to the class: the first covered countries the Nazis occupied and the fictional characters and settings each student created. They chose victims, bystanders or perpetrators, all designed around historical accuracy. Finally, they wrote research papers that examined hypotheses from a vast number of Holocaust issues and events. Piri was impressed with the students' growing knowledge and creativity, and she became more comfortable about speaking publicly for the first time.

Clearly, the students, most of whom had little knowledge about the Holocaust before taking the course, were prepared for Piri's discussion. (Years later, when *Shadows* was published, the students read and discussed the book and asked Piri to sign their copies, which she did with self-conscious humility; and on April 6, 1994 a University- and community-wide *Yom Hashoah,* Holocaust Remembrance day conference was held, planned by students from my class. Piri worked on the planning committee and was a featured speaker. The incident that occurred at the end of her lecture that day is recounted in this volume and continues to inspire questions of fate and life's great mysteries.)

The students were deeply interested in meeting Piri. She impressed them as someone who, despite her suffering, had an enduring faith in the ultimate goodness of people. She spoke passionately about her loving family and painfully about her suffering and the murders she witnessed at the hands of her Nazi captors. When she paused and invited the students to ask the questions they prepared, Piri answered without reservation, even those questions that were intimate. When asked if she forgave the Nazis for their actions, she said, "No. There are some actions that are unforgivable." She willingly showed the students the numbers tattooed on her forearm in Auschwitz and said, "I will never have them removed. They are a reminder of the worst in human behavior and the lessons we must learn from the Holocaust."

Piri spoke to my students every year, recounting her personal story, adding a dimension to Holocaust studies that only a survivor can relate. Since my retirement, Dr. Sigmar Schwarz teaches the class and Piri speaks to his students each year. In addition to the Holocaust course, Piri lectures in classes across the University's curriculum in which intolerance is a topic of discussion: in English, sociology, psychology, philosophy, women's studies, religion and criminal justice. She speaks, too, at Moorpark College, in public schools in the region, and has been interviewed over the years by local newspapers. Even when ill health has challenged her, Piri gathers her strength to speak to the students. "It is my duty," she tells them.

Piri has been a presence on campus since 1989. She audits courses in a variety of subjects and has found a place that satisfies her love of knowledge and her desire to inform students about the darkest period in human history. And there are the people who have altered her life. "I have so many friends at CLU," Piri told me recently, friends among faculty and students, even among students who have graduated, who write to Piri and meet the Bodnars for lunch in nearby restaurants and at their homes.

In 2002 the University to which Piri is so devoted and which she calls "my second home" honored her with an award for her service to CLU's students. The award ceremony was a surprise, the only way, Zoli said, he could get her to go, for her modesty would prevent her from accepting an award for doing what she sees as a gift of the heart.

. . . .

In the spring of 1988, Piri and Zoli returned to her childhood home in Miscolc, Hungary. The cherry trees that she so adored as a child were in bloom, their petals drifting onto her father's grave just as they had when Piri was a girl. She saw in the survival of her beloved cherry trees her own survival, a symbol of hope at the heart of Piri's vision for peace.

This dual memoir, and the poetry included here, take the reader on a journey to Hungary where two loving families were plunged into the upside-down world of the Holocaust. Their survival has brought them *Out of the Shadows* and into the light of what Piri prays will be a more respectful and kinder world.

Marsha Carow Markman, Ph.D.
Professor Emeritus, English Department
March 1, 2006

Foreword

The events that led to the loss of eleven million lives began on January 30, 1933, when Adolf Hitler and the National Socialist German Workers' Party came to power. Hitler, an Austrian by birth, won support for the Nazi party by promising glory to Germany after years of depression and the loss of World War I.

Hitler's plan to win power for Germany was based in large degree on his belief in the superiority and purity of the Aryan race and, by extension, of the German people. Although he considered Gypsies, Russians, Poles, and other Slavic people inferior, he focused on the Jews, whom he intended to eliminate in Germany and ultimately in all of Europe. The Nazis' "Final Solution to the Jewish Question" supported that intention.

The Nazis were fanatically devoted to Hitler's racial program and, as a result, Germany fought World War II on two fronts: on the field of battle against the Allies, and against the Jews in the countries Germany occupied. That second battle also included converts to Christianity if the Nazis deemed there were genetic links to their Jewish heritage. So fanatical was this second war that, even when it was clear that the first battle was lost, the second continued on.

The process by which the Nazis aimed to achieve their goals included: identification of Jews, their elimination from social and economic life, forced labor, and forced transport to labor, concentration, and death camps. This process was repeated throughout occupied Europe, and culminated with the murder of approximately six million Jews—nearly two-thirds of Europe's Jews and one-third of the Jews of the world. It is important to note that, while there were individuals in every country throughout occupied Europe who supported the Nazis, there were also courageous individual and underground movements that rescued Jews.

Hungary's ebb-and-flow history of anti-Semitism, rested upon the country's leadership, its economy, and the effects of war and revised boundaries, specifically following World War I. Pro-Nazi sentiment and Hungary's alliance with Nazi Germany, saw an increase in anti-Jewish sanctions. Those sanctions grew from limiting employment opportunities to— beginning in 1938—depriving Jews of legal and civil rights, and excluding them from cultural activities and from participation in the economy.

Jewish schools and synagogues were closed and often destroyed; and businesses owned by Jews were confiscated. In 1939 a labor service law created the *Munkaszologalat,*a forced-labor system for Jewish men.

Forty-two thousand Hungarian Jews perished in those forced-labor units prior to the German occupation.

On March 19, 1944, German forces occupied Hungary; and by April 5, 1944, Hungarian authorities enforced anti-Jewish decrees, completing the isolation and identification of the country's Jews. Businesses and properties were confiscated, and Jews were required to wear the six-pointed Star of David on their outer clothing.

On April 16th of that year, the first day of Passover, the concentration of Hungarian Jews began. Local gendarmes and the notorious Arrow Cross, known for cruelty and anti-Semitism, moved thousands of Jews into ghettos. From there, they were transported to labor, concentration, and death camps.

At the same time, Germany was facing defeat on all fronts. The Americans had landed at Normandy and Soviet forces had crossed the Romanian border. Nevertheless, the German plan for total extermination of the Jews proceeded in Hungary with lightning speed.

The Nazis, with the aid of enormous manpower and machinery, forced approximately 435,000 Hungarian Jews onto cattle trains between May 15, 1944 and July 9, 1944. There they faced cruelty and certain death in the gas chambers of Auschwitz-Birkenau, the most notorious of Europe's death camps. Thus the process of identification, confiscation, isolation, and deportation was complete. Only annihilation remained.

Auschwitz-Birkenau is approximately thirty miles west of Krakow, Poland. The entire camp had a capacity of four million people, but by the end of the war it was crowded beyond its capacity. The Nazis divided the camp into three sections. Auschwitz I was an administrative center and a concentration camp. Birkenau was the death camp. Its four crematoria, with forty-six ovens, exterminated about five thousand persons each day. With the ovens straining to meet impossible quotas, people were murdered and buried in large pits.

Manowitz was a third part of the camp, and provided slave labor for a synthetic rubber plant, Buna, built by the I.G. Farben Corporation. Up to one hundred persons a day were worked to death in Manowitz.

Most of the Jews deported from Hungary died in the gas chambers shortly after their arrival at Auschwitz. Nazi Germany's "Final Solution" resulted in the murder of approximately 560,000 Hungarian Jews, nearly 70 percent of Hungary's Jewish population.

Piri and Zoltan Bodnar are Hungarian Jews who survived the Nazi death camps. Their stories are replete with torture and the loss of loved ones at the hands of their captors. They will forever carry with them the physical and emotional pain that they experienced and witnessed—testimony to the worst genocide in recorded history. Hope, faith, and luck helped them to survive and to build a new family and a new life together. Yet, they cannot put their Holocaust experiences aside, painful as they are to recount. They must testify to the abominations that we are capable of committing when hate is taken to its extreme. The experiences they relate here are incredulous, but their message is clear if we take heed:

> We cannot hate; we must not hate,
> We cannot forget; we must not forget.

Dana J. Cordero
Marsha C. Markman

TABLE OF CONTENTS

In the Shadow of Death

Horror presides over the camp
We hear the victims' dreadful cry
Young and old, righteous and wise
Marching to their deaths tonight

Tear-soaked faces, bewildered eyes
Children trembling and petrified
Babies torn from their mothers' arms
Heaven and earth clashing tonight

Parents tormented, beg the guards
Have mercy on our precious ones
They are so frail, weak and small
Please, don't hurt them, grant them life

The gas chamber locked, the shower starts
The victims are choking, losing their minds
Scratching the wall, screaming and crawl
But no way out, no place to hide

Naked bodies with vacant eyes
Dumped on each other in a cart
Their torture ended, their pain is gone
The soul's eternal journey begun

The flames are coiling toward the sky
The martyrs' ashes cover the ground
smoke fills up the deadly night
And the massacre goes on and on

We live each moment in terror and fear
The angel of death always so near
Loved ones perish in front of our eyes
Our world is crumbling, but we strive to survive.

Piri Piroska Bodnar

ZOLI'S STORY

Szendro: The Early Years

Szendro when I was a boy, was a charming, agricultural town in Hungary with a population of 5,000. The majority of the people was Catholic with a minority of Methodists, Evangelists, Presbyterians and Jehovah's Witnesses. There were also 240 Jewish people in the town, but regardless of religious beliefs, people lived next to each other in relative harmony and helped one another when in need.

The town was embraced by lush green rolling hills and a beautiful forest. The outskirts of Szendro were made up of rich, fertile lands with wheat and cornfields as well as pastures for cattle and sheep. From early spring through autumn, the countryside was ablaze with colorful wildflowers.

My mother and father were born into this tranquil environment. As children, my parents were neighbors and often played together. And with the passage of time their friendship turned into love. They were both still quite young—by today's standards—when their love finally reached its culmination. My mother, Ilonka, was a beautiful, 16-year-old girl with long, wavy black hair, violet eyes and a flawless complexion. She was also slightly overweight, which was fashionable in that era. My 18-year-old father, Lajos, was a dashing young man with jet-black hair, olive skin and sky-blue eyes.

3

When the young couple expressed their desire to be married they were met with rejection from both families. My mother was raised by Orthodox Jewish parents and my father's parents were devoted Catholics. At the turn of the century, interfaith marriages were extremely rare in Hungary, especially in small towns and villages. But the young lovers didn't give up hope.

My father realized that the only way he could marry his sweetheart was by converting to Judaism, a decision that took tremendous courage and sacrifice. His parents were disappointed and fiercely opposed his abandoning the religion he had been born into and practiced for eighteen years. However, against their will, my father began the long and difficult process of conversion.

Szendro had a Jewish school, a *Yeshiva*, and one of its former students became my father's teacher. Every night after work he went for his lessons. He was an excellent student, eager to learn and within two years he finished his studies. He became fluent in reading and understanding Hebrew and became knowledgeable about the *Talmud* and the history of the Jewish people. But in order to become a full-fledged Jew, he had one more task to accomplish. At the age of twenty, he went to Budapest and in a Jewish hospital he was circumcised.

My mother was eighteen and my father twenty when they married in December 1924. The entire Jewish community was invited and celebrated their marriage. Unfortunately, my father's family boycotted the happy occasion.

The young couple settled down in Szendro and began their married life in the same one-room-and-kitchen adobe house where my mother and her mother before her were born. However, my parents lived with my maternal grandparents for only a short time before they moved into their own home. My mother added to the couple's income by embroidering sheets and tablecloths for prospective brides, while my father, leaving his shoemaking trade, became a businessman.

From wealthy local peasants, he bought acres of forestland and, with the help of a few day laborers, cut down the trees and sold the timber to lumber yards and to the railroad. My father always worked alongside his men and they loved him for his honesty and kindness.

His in-laws adored him, treating him as if he were their son. Although he became a devoted Jew, he never ignored or forgot his roots. He kept a close relationship with his parents, brother, sisters and childhood friends, despite their opposition to his conversion.

The people of Szendro lived a simple life. Most of them grew their own vegetables, had a few fruit trees, and raised chickens and geese. (Some who were considered wealthy raised pigs, lambs, cows and horses.) However, there were items—such as sugar, salt, tea, spices, candles, rice soap, and kerosene—that were purchased from the local, family-owned grocery store.

Every household was lit with kerosene lamps, and the stoves fed with firewood or coal. There was no electricity, indoor plumbing, gas, or telephone service. Food was stored in a cellar or dark room, and water was carried in buckets from a distant well, half of it spilling out on the way home. In order to save numerous trips to the well, people took a bath only once a week and changed their underclothes at the same time. In addition, very few people, including my mother and father owned a toothbrush or toothpaste, items that were considered luxuries that only the rich could afford. Needless to say, sanitary conditions were extremely poor; and the outhouses were overrun with flies, worms and other insects that carried contagious diseases.

The town had no movie theaters, library, parks, clubs or restaurants. Instead, people relied on each other for entertainment. The tavern was the most popular gathering place for the men. There, they drank and often fought, both verbally and physically. Two churches and two synagogues in the town

5

provided places where people worshipped and socialized on Saturday and Sunday, as well as on holy days.

Married women were expected to stay at home, raise their children, cook, clean and do the laundry (by hand, since there were no washing machines). They were also responsible for feeding the livestock and cultivating the vegetable gardens. In their spare hours—which were few—they visited friends and neighbors where they would knit, sew and gossip.

Among Szendro's residents was Dr. Sandor Zoltan, the town's only physician, who was also a Jew. He was a compassionate, dedicated man. On call twenty-four hours a day, seven days a week, Dr. Zoltan cared for the town's five thousand residents, as well as the three thousand people in the surrounding villages. In rainstorm, in snowstorm and in below-zero temperatures, he visited the sick in his horse and buggy.

Most of his patients couldn't pay for the doctor's services. Yet, he never refused to treat anyone who needed his help. He was a poor man as far as material wealth was concerned, but he was rich in blessings and love, which the people showered on him. Although he never expected to be paid by those who were poverty-stricken, occasionally they would bring him two or three eggs or a handful of corn. He truly believed that it is better to give than to receive, and his actions emulated his beliefs.

In this poor town were a few wealthy landowners who socialized only among themselves, giving elaborate parties for their rich and influential friends, and for visiting dignitaries. Meanwhile their servants, along with their families and most of Szendro's population, lived in extreme poverty.

I was born on March 19, 1925. I came into the world in the same house—and the same bed—as my mother did nineteen years earlier. The Jewish community was overwhelmed by my birth. I was the first Jewish child in Szendro with a Jewish mother and a former Catholic father. My father was proud of me and would often take me to visit his parents, sisters and brother.

I was a strong-willed, free-spirited child, with a great love for people, animals and the outdoors; and I lived in a town that was safe for adults and for children like me who wandered and explored. If we children got lost, for example, the town was alerted and someone would deliver us home.

I would often drop by a neighbor's home for a visit and was always welcomed. Gentiles frequently asked me jokingly, "Zoli, what are you: a Jew or a Christian?" I would answer them, "From the waist down I am a Jew and from the waist up I am a Christian." They always laughed and rewarded my answer with cookies or candy.

One day, when I was only three, I decided to visit my maternal grandparents whose home was a ten-minute walk from our house. It was a cold winter morning so my mother bundled me up in warm clothing and told me to go straight to Grandma's home.

As I was strolling along the road, the laughter and frolicking of a group of children captured my attention. The boys were sliding down a hill on a sleigh and seemed to be having a jolly time. I stood mesmerized by their merriment and wished that I could join them in their fun. But they were much older than me and I was too intimidated to approach them. As the day wore on, snowflakes began to fall and it became extremely cold. The icy wind howled like a pack of wolves; but I didn't hear or see anything except the children's laughter and smiling faces.

The day faded into dusk. It was dinnertime and my mother was sure that I was in Grandma's warm kitchen. But when my father came home and I was still out, she became worried and came looking for me. She found me shivering on the frozen ground where I had stood for eight hours. Both of my feet were frozen and I couldn't move. My mother carried me home where

I remained in bed for six months with hypothermia and oozing infections in my feet.

From that adventurous day on, whenever the weather became chilly and snow began to fall, it meant a few weeks in bed for me. Later in my life I realized the high price I paid for my childhood adventure.

April 10, 1928, was one of the happiest days in my life. On that glorious day my precious brother, Imre, was born. He became my most trusted and cherished friend. Because he was several years younger than me, we had different groups of friends; nevertheless, we spent a great deal of time together. Like any siblings, however, we would occasionally argue and fight; but we loved each other dearly. Imre, my soft-spoken brother, was a loving son and a compassionate human being. Little did I know that our lives together would be so brief.

At the age of six my grade school and my Jewish-school education began. My morning hours were spent in the classroom learning to read and write; and following a lunch break, my studies continued in Hebrew school.

Public school, however, was an unpleasant place. My teacher was a hot-tempered, impatient woman whose pets were the rich boys and girls. I felt like a prisoner in the classroom and it was no small wonder that I took every opportunity to escape from my "cell."

In Hebrew school, too, my teacher was strict, and expected the impossible from six- and seven-year-old children. However, I made many friends in school and among them was my best friend, Volu. He and I were mischievous and adventurous. As a result, we were always getting into trouble. Together we went hiking, swimming and mud bathing. We were inseparable, and not a day passed that we didn't spend at least a few hours together.

Sabbath was my favorite day and even after seven decades, I can still see my mother preparing the holiday dinner. Just before the candles were lit, we bathed and dressed in clean, pressed clothing. This holiest night of the week, with its prayers, special foods and loving family, is forever engraved in the bank of my memory.

Saturday morning my brother and I joined our father and grandfather at the synagogue. After the service my friends and I gathered in the temple courtyard to discuss our plans for the rest of the day. We had many places from which to choose, but two that we all agreed upon: One was an abandoned, ancient fortress at the top of a grassy hill. The whole area was overgrown with weeds and cobwebs like delicate gray lace hanging from tree branches and covering the ground. The fortress was hidden from human eyes by mature trees. In the middle of its courtyard was a large pit where we sat in a circle telling ghost stories. It was a world of our own, far from parental supervision—a mystical, magical hideaway.

The second place was a beautiful forest about two miles outside of town. When the winter snow melted and spring was in the air, my friends and I spent many happy hours among its towering trees. It was a peaceful haven for people as well as animals. The forest was filled with the melodies of larks and robins. Woodpeckers feasted on the trees while humming birds zipped about searching for nectar; and occasionally a bear would be lured by the many fruits and nuts available. For us children the forest was a veritable feast of raspberries, strawberries, blueberries and nuts of all kinds. Almost everything in the forest was good to eat except the mushrooms, which were poisonous. I still recall vividly the magical times my friends and I spent in our forest paradise.

The 1930s brought hard times to the entire world and Hungary was not excluded. The country was hit hard by the failing economy and unemployment was steadily rising. Thousands of people lost their jobs, businesses, homes and their life savings. Unable to provide for their families, many people turned to alcohol to drown their helplessness.

On a windy, autumn day in 1932, I was working in the garden with my father when a man came looking for Lajos Bodnar.

"He is not home," said my father. "But he will return within two weeks." It was a God-sent miracle that I didn't utter a word. When the man left, I asked my father, "Daddy, why did you say that you weren't home?"

With tears in his eyes, he embraced me and said: "My precious child, if I had told the truth, the tax collector would have taken everything we own." But my father was an intensely honest man and lying to the tax collector hurt him deeply. So he made a promise to himself to pay back taxes he owed, even though he would have to work even harder to earn the needed money. True to his word, my father repaid the overdue taxes within two weeks. After that incident he frequently reminded me that I should always tell the truth no matter how painful the consequences might be. And throughout my life I've followed his advice.

Until 1936, Szendro was largely unaffected by the growing anti-Semitism in Hungary. However, more and more wealthy Christians began to send their children to the cities to be educated. These students returned home for the holidays and summer vacation with vicious lies about the Jews, blaming us for the catastrophe that hit the country. In addition, young hoodlums distributed fliers with deadly slogans that read:

"Jews are pigs!"

"Jews don't belong in Hungary!"

"Let's free the country from the Jews!"

"Jews go home to Palestine!"

These hoodlums were the educated children of the wealthy villagers. Unfortunately for us Jews, most of the village people believed whatever the students told them, so enamored were they of their education. These hoodlums convinced the simple town's folk with their poisonous propaganda; and many city officials and clergymen, as well as others in the community, accepted the students' distorted notions and also expressed their distrust and dislike for the town's Jews.

While anti-Semitism existed before this time, it became more prevalent throughout the country, sweeping through its towns and villages. People needed scapegoats, and who were better suited to take the blame for all the problems in Hungary than the Jews? We couldn't believe the accusations made against us. Every word they uttered was filled with hate but welcomed by the majority of the people who, it was rumored, would receive land and other property owned by the Jews if we were gone—a most enticing promise, particularly for the poor amongst us. Needless to say, the Jews were a minority in Hungary with no political power with which to strike back.

We were heartbroken, for we were taught in school as well as at home to love our country. We were proud of Hungary—it was our home. We were born, raised and educated there. And we Jews had a long and rich history in Hungary. Our ancestors stretched back a thousand years and our people contributed a great deal to the country's economy. Physicians, scientists, scholars in so many fields, and philanthropists were respected Jews; and now we were being told that we were the enemies of the country—the country we loved.

As the weeks and months passed, life became increasingly difficult for us. The once peaceful, friendly place of my birth was rapidly disappearing. Many of our neighbors whom we trusted and loved turned their backs on us. They avoided us on the street, behaving as if they had never known us. Former friends became greedy and wanted the property that the rumors had promised them. We were deeply hurt by their attitudes and behavior and realized that we stood alone in what was to be the darkest period in human history.

Fascist youths in the cities organized the "Arrow Cross" and, working outside government sanctions, terrorized the Jews. Additionally, in 1938 Hungary's Nazi officials ordered all Jewish businesses closed or handed over to their gentile employees without any financial compensation. These sanctions against the Hungarian Jews were similar to those against the Jews in Germany.

In 1939, following junior high school graduation, I decided to learn a trade. My parents were disappointed and tried to persuade me to continue my education; however, they were unsuccessful. We had a distant relative in Miskolc, a town thirty-eight kilometers from Szendro, who persuaded my parents to let me come to the city and be an apprentice in his three-chair barbershop. It took several weeks before my parents finally agreed to let me go assured, however, that I would return home within a week or two.

The night before my departure, my friends gave me a farewell party and the following morning they joined my family and me at the railroad station. When my brother embraced and kissed me, my heart ached and tears began to choke me; but I suppressed my emotion, for this was to be the beginning of my life's work.

As the train pulled out of the station, I took one last glance at the flowering countryside where I had spent a carefree childhood, the happiest years of my young life. I was leaving behind the green hills and colorful meadows, the dusty, unpaved roads of Szendro, and my beloved parents and brother. But I would carry all of those memories with me forever.

Miskolc 1939

Before my journey began, it was decided that I would reside with my employer, his wife, and their five children. Their two-bedroom, kitchen apartment was overcrowded and its only luxury was electricity. It was the first time that I was away from home and I cried myself to sleep many nights. But I never let anyone see my tears. No one knew how homesick I was or how much I missed my family and friends. To ease my yearning for them I buried myself in work.

Miskolc was home to 75,000 people, most of whom were barely able to feed and clothe their families. Many of them lived in overcrowded apartments, which they often shared with five or six family members. The kitchen was used for cooking, sleeping and bathing; and the outhouse was shared with other tenants. In the absence of trashcans, the remnants of vegetables, dirty dishwater and other garbage were thrown out into the courtyard. Especially during the summer, the stench of rotten garbage became a lure for insects and rats.

A muddy yard, shared among the tenants of three apartment buildings, was the children's playground; but there was no grass, no flowers and no toys, books, or money for the movies or other entertainment. Indeed, there was no beauty, nothing to offset the bleak environment in which ugliness and misery were constant companions.

To add to this wretchedness was the ridicule to which the Jewish children were subjected, often in response to their tattered and patched clothing and shoes. Surely the abuse left an everlasting scar upon them. Despite the poverty, the Jewish families made many sacrifices for their children. They encouraged them to excel in school as well as in life. And while anti-Semitism was a presence long before the Nazis came into power, the Jewish children, myself included, somehow dealt with the increase that its ideology wrought. Many times when we walked home from school we were met by gentile school children who called us "dirty Jew" and pulled on our side curls. The emotional abuse caused ceaseless pain, along with a keen awareness that we Jews were different from the gentiles.

While most of the citizens of Miskolc lived in poverty, there were several rich families in the town, nearly all of them Christians. It was difficult then (and impossible later) for a Jew to own property in Hungary, especially in the overcrowded towns and cities. We therefore "earned" an undeserved reputation by them for being lazy, poor and dirty. Needless to say, there was a large social division between the rich and the poor; and the rich, with their wealth, were generally able to bend the laws, even mistreat Jews and avoid the consequences of their actions. Unfortunately, the police rarely favored a Jew in these circumstances.

During my first year as an apprentice for my uncle, my main responsibilities consisted of cleaning the shop, brushing hair off the customers, running errands and delivering groceries to my employer's home. My uncle taught me very little about the trade of being a barber, but it was common practice for first-year apprentices to be used as errand boys. Nevertheless, I watched my uncle at work whenever I could; and in this way I learned about cutting hair.

My parents took every opportunity, during that first year, to visit me and to make sure that I was well and cared for. I cherished those few hours that I spent with my loved ones. Although I had no vacation time, I went home when I could, even if for only a few hours, to be with my family and friends.

In my second year as an apprentice, my employer and the journeyman were both drafted into the army and decided, as a result, to close the shop. I was desperate because I loved my intended trade, and therefore tried to persuade my employer to let me run the business.

"Uncle Alex," I said. "Please don't close down the place, I'm able to take care of it." He looked at me with disbelief.

"What are you talking about, Zoli? You have no experience in cutting hair or running a barber shop."

I was tenacious in my response: "You are wrong, Uncle. I have a great deal of experience." I said. "For quite a while I've been cutting my friends' hair at their homes after work. And every morning before you come into the shop, I've brought in unemployed, homeless men and given them haircuts and shaves at no charge. They are grateful for the free service. But actually I am the one who benefited from them. So you see Uncle I'm capable of doing this job." After listening to my plea he said, "You are right Zoli; what can I lose?" So at the tender age of fifteen, I became the sole supporter of a family of seven: paying the rent for the shop and apartment, buying the groceries and paying all of their bills. My work ethic was impeccable and I took my responsibilities seriously—a trait I had learned from my father.

At first the customers hesitated to sit down for me and would jokingly ask, "Zoli should we call the ambulance before you start shaving?" Luckily there was never a need for that. I tried my utmost and succeeded in running my Uncle's shop well.

One year later, when my employer returned from army duty, he was astonished to learn that not only had he not lost a single customer, but had gained many new ones. There were tears in his eyes as he embraced me and thanked me for taking care of his family and the business. By the time I was sixteen years old, I was a master barber, a trade that would later become my livelihood.

__The Beginning of the Labor Camps__

It was in the spring of 1940, when a new high official, Ivan Nemeth, arrived in Szendro. Little did we know about the enormous hate this man held for Jews. Soon after settling down in his office he designed a plan to make our lives miserable. Nemeth issued a proclamation stating that every Jewish man between the ages of fourteen and sixty must report for duty in a forced labor camp.

On a golden autumn day, a letter arrived from home informing me that my father must report to such a labor camp. I took the first train home to bid him farewell. With a few belongings in a knapsack, he tearfully embraced us. We clung to him, crying, not wanting to let go.

Our world had suddenly crumbled; my mother and brother were left without a source of income as were so many other Jewish families. Winter was approaching and the money my mother earned by embroidering pillowcases and tablecloths was hardly enough for even the barest of necessities. However, I made a promise to my father that I would look after my mother and brother. Fortunately, I was able to keep that promise by working extra hours.

The first letter we received from my father came from the Salgotarjan slave labor camp where he was forced to work for a few short weeks. His unit was then shifted from camp to camp, but as long as he was in Hungary we were able to communicate with him through the mail and were allowed to visit him.

One day during my visit, my father's lieutenant called him into his office.

"Bodnar," said the officer. "You are Catholic by birth and don't have to go through this hell. I am giving you twenty-four hours to return to your town and bring back your birth certificate and you will be a free man."

"Will it help my family too?" asked my father.

"Unfortunately, it will not," said the lieutenant. "Your children were born to a Jewish mother and therefore they are Jews."

"Thank you very much Lieutenant," said my father. "But I will take the same fate and will endure the same hardships as my family."

I begged my father to reconsider and tried to persuade him to follow logic, not his heart. But all to no avail.

"I will never give in to the Hungarian Nazis," was his answer.

My father's last letter to my brother and me came from Budapest:

"My battalion is being transferred to Ukrania, but I hope that fate will bring us together very soon. Take care of each other, my dearest, and never lose faith in God."

After a few weeks in Ukrania, his battalion was taken to the Russian front, where the men shoveled coal along the railroad routes. One day, my father encountered one of his closest childhood friends, Karpus Tamas. Tamas, a Christian, was in the Hungarian army but was still loyal to the friendship he had with my father. Despite the danger, that wonderful man helped my father in every way he could. When he came home for leave, he brought news of my father and when returning to the front, he brought food and warm clothing to him.

German Troops Occupy Hungary

In spite of the difficulties of the time, I was young, filled with ambition and dreams, and passionately in love with life. One of my great passions was dancing, and every Saturday and Sunday night—and sometimes even after work—I went to the dance hall. It was wartime and the songs were about the uncertainty and fragility of life. Their lyrics encouraged the young people to live each moment to the fullest. (Many teenagers and young adults responded by engaging in sexual activities that, under normal circumstances, would not have been acceptable.)

The dance hall was a place for young people to congregate, to dance and to forget the horror of the war that was sweeping through Europe. After the initial advance on Austria, German troops conquered and occupied country after country, marching through cities, towns and villages. They would leave behind misery, grief, death and mass graves.

Although we heard about the atrocities of Hitler's Germany, we simply couldn't believe that it would affect us in Hungary. Ignorance of all of the facts, as well as denial, were no doubt the reason for our disbelief, because it was evident that the majority of high ranking Hungarian officials, as well as thousands of ordinary people, sympathized with the Nazis. We should have known that it was only a matter of time before Hungary would joyfully welcome the German troops into the country.

It was March 19, 1944, my nineteenth birthday, and the long harsh winter days had finally come to an end. Snow flowers, violets and lilies of the fields began to appear on the meadows. I woke up early, as usual, to get ready for work—looking forward to the day and the later activities of the night. Since it was my birthday, my friends had planned a party to celebrate the happy occasion. I tried to push the time, waiting anxiously for the fun-filled night. But when night finally arrived, I was unaware of what it had in store for me—an event that would change my life forever.

The sky was adorned with dazzling stars; and I hurriedly dressed to meet my friends for dinner. After a delightful dinner we went dancing in a hall brightly lit by a crystal chandelier. Steve—a blind man—played beautiful melodies on a battered piano. We danced and sang, enjoying the splendor of the night.

Suddenly, one of my friends, who was listening to the radio, shouted for us to hear: German troops had occupied Hungary. The music stopped, the dance hall became quiet and everyone stood still in shock. It took only a few minutes to digest the horrible news. My friends and I left the hall in a state of panic, trying desperately to deny what had come true.

On March 27, 1944, eight days after the German occupation, a proclamation was issued stating that every Jew must wear a canary-yellow Star on all visible garments. We were branded like cattle and became a target for anyone who wished to abuse us. And abused we were: mentally, physically and spiritually. No one came to our rescue and no law protected us.

Whenever I went outside I wore a raincoat thrown over my shoulder to hide my yellow star. It was foolish of me and very risky. If an Arrow Cross member recognized me I could have been killed. But, like many other young people, I took my chances.

A Fateful Choice

After Germany occupied Hungary, life became even worse for the Jews. The Nazis seized all Jewish property, including homes, and forced all Jews into ghettos on the outskirts of towns. The ghettos were even more miserable, crowded and dirtier than the impoverished neighborhood we lived in before. The only way out, however, was to work outside the city in a labor camp, an option that seemed better than imprisonment in the ghetto. So I, along with many young and middle-aged Jewish men, volunteered for work outside the ghetto. We were taken to Salgotarjan's labor camp, where we worked as lumberjacks. Our jobs were strenuous: unloading wood from freight cars and carrying sacks of wheat almost as heavy as we were. We worked hard, but were treated humanely. The food was good and plentiful and we slept in clean stables.

Our lives changed drastically in the beginning of May 1944, however, when we were transported to the Joshua forced labor camp. The officer in charge, Lieutenant Josza, was an evil person who enjoyed ultimate power over us. With whip in hand and revolver in holster, he was one of the most feared individuals in the camp. Mercy and compassion were unknown to him.

I was delegated camp barber, so I didn't go outside to work. However, one day I learned that my brother, Imre, was in a nearby labor camp. I decided to join him and asked permission for a transfer, but I was refused. The desire to be united with my brother was overwhelming, and there was no sacrifice too great and no obstacle that could prevent me from achieving my goal. On one stormy night, I packed my belongings and escaped. At the time, there were only a few guards, and no barbed wire surrounding the camp; the Nazis kept up the charade that we were there as laborers, not prisoners. It was easy to escape and sneak into the other camp under the cover of darkness.

My brother and I had a tearful reunion and we promised each other that we would never part. Once again I became the camp barber, but I asked permission to go out to work in the fields alongside my brother and friends. The camp director granted my wish; but after work I still had to fulfill my obligation as a barber.

Each morning as we were going out to work we encountered a group of well-dressed, well-fed Jewish girls. They were sitting in comfortable carriages guarded by young hoodlums, heading toward the elegant villas that the Nazis had confiscated from the Jews. The girls were used as housekeepers, cooks, seamstresses and sex slaves. They lived in comfortable apartments and were well fed and treated humanely. But one day the girls disappeared and no one knew what happened to them. It would be much later that I would learn their fate.

Journey to Camp 11

It was October 12, 1944. The rainy season was upon us as our journey toward an uncertain destination began. There were 240 of us—mostly young, healthy men in our teens and early twenties. That morning at daybreak we were roused harshly from our bunks. Following a breakfast of bread, cheese and coffee, the march began, with no indication where we were going.

On our path we frequently met people from all walks of life: factory workers going to work, peasants sitting on ox-pulled wagons heading to town to sell their stock on the open market, herdsmen with their cattle and shepherds with their sheep.

We passed tiny villages, towns, rain-soaked fields and wooded areas, their golden leaves beneath our feet. We envied those people whom we encountered, for they were free. They had no guards with rifles watching their every step. At nightfall they went home to their loved ones, to a roof over their heads. No matter how simple and hard their lives were, they were blessed by the most precious of gifts—denied to us—*freedom*. Freedom many of us didn't appreciate until it was lost.

Lieutenant Josza was still in command; he sat in a comfortable carriage pulled by a beautiful white horse. His immense hatred for us made him a beast. He would often step down from his carriage and, whip in hand, begin beating us without provocation. He would then climb back into his carriage and take to the road once again.

At midday, the troop always stopped for a short lunch break—hardly enough for a rest—and then we would continue the march until nightfall. For nearly two weeks there was an ever-present rain cloud in the autumn sky and the weather became colder with each passing day. There was thunder and lightning, followed inevitably by rainstorms.

As a result of the soaking rain and the continued forced marching, the soles and heels of our shoes became worn. Mud and water entered through the holes, making the march increasingly difficult. To make the journey more bearable, we began to discard some of the possessions from our backpacks. At each stop we left behind essential items and kept only a few pairs of underwear, sweaters, blankets and priceless family pictures. I was determined, however, to carry my barber tools with me, hoping I would be lucky enough to use them.

Every day, after an exhausting fifteen-mile march, when darkness enveloped us, we stopped for the night. Usually two of our guards were sent ahead to find sleeping quarters for us. Occasionally, if we were fortunate, we were sheltered in barns or abandoned homesteads. But most often we slept under the cold, cloudy sky. Following the evening meals, which became smaller and smaller as time passed, we turned in for the night. The hay and straw kept us warm and sleep came quickly; but dawn arrived much too soon and another day of misery began.

Sometimes when we spent the night on a farm we were allowed to ask the farmer if we could buy some food, but the farmers seldom agreed. They usually cursed and screamed at us:

"Go to Hell you rotten Jews!" they shouted. "We would like to see all of you starve to death!"

We didn't know at the time that their death wish would come true. But what was our crime? If being a Jew was an unforgivable crime, then we were guilty of the charge.

Our next stop was the city of Hatvan and in spite of the rain we were put to work at a railroad station, feeding German locomotives. We were forced into the backbreaking labor of shoveling tons of coal into the massive German trains that, unlike modern electric trains, needed to burn the fuel to run. Hungarian soldiers, with bayonets and rifles in hand, were in charge of us. They were brutal, bloodthirsty individuals who were anxious to kill us whenever possible. We stayed in Hatvan for six weeks before our miserable march to Budapest began.

It was a long two weeks' walk with barely enough food to keep us alive, and a march made even more difficult by the rocky, hilly terrain. Many of the men in our group collapsed from exhaustion, hunger and illness; the rest of us forced ourselves to go on. Nevertheless, death was a constant companion along the way. Since my brother and I were young and stronger than most of the others—and were from the countryside—we fared better in the foul weather and under the dreadful circumstances. Even so, we covered many miles leaning on each other for physical and emotional support.

When we finally reached the city of Budapest, we were held in a vacant school building enclosed by a high cement wall. Hungarian hoodlums were in charge of us and clearly enjoyed their power. We very soon heard rumors, which turned out to be true, that the city had a few safe houses where Jews could find refuge from the murderers. When darkness cloaked the city, a few prisoners attempted to escape and many of them succeeded. We had nothing to lose and I decided that escape was worth the risk.

I told my brother about my plan to escape and tried to persuade him to join me. I knew it was a dangerous undertaking but it was worth a try. But my brother, a country boy of fifteen who had never been outside his birthplace, was afraid. However, when he saw how determined I was he said, "Zoli, you go first and I will follow you shortly." He encouraged me to make the attempt to escape and promised to meet up with me within three hours at a designated place a short distance from the compound. As I hugged and kissed him, I was torn between leaving him behind and staying with him.

Darkness crept over the city and the sky was covered with rain clouds as I headed toward the eight-foot wall. Within the wall were crevices and broken pieces of cement which a few of my comrades had used as hand-and-foot holds to climb the wall and escape. Guards walked up and down the large yard and occasionally engaged in conversation with other guards. Luck was with me as I ran toward the wall without being noticed. After a short, tense moment of struggle I started my climb without being noticed. My hands searched for crevices in the wall's face, and soon were bruised and bloodied, but years of rock climbing with my friends served me well and I quickly climbed to the top of the wall and jumped down to the street below.

There was a large apartment building nearby and I ran to the entrance and stood under its awning. I knew that the city had a thousand eyes and it would only take one person to spot me and report to the SS, so I took off my armband with its yellow Star of David and placed it in my coat pocket.

At four o'clock in the morning it was dark with no moon or stars visible in the sky; without hesitation I went to our meeting place. Each minute seemed like an eternity as I waited for my brother. An hour went by, then two, then three and there was still no sign of him. I became panicky and realized that my brother wouldn't be able to escape. My few short hours of freedom were heavenly, but I had a duty to my brother.

My mind was made up to return to the compound for I wouldn't abandon Imre whom I dearly loved. So I climbed the wall once again and left liberty behind. As soon as the guards saw me they said that they had been looking for me for hours. They took me to the Lieutenant who was waiting for me with furious, murderous eyes.

"You son of a bitch," he yelled at me. "You will pay with your life for trying to escape." I was dragged outside and shoved up against the cement wall that only a few hours before led to my freedom. The Lieutenant drew his revolver and placed it against my head. I was terrified, shaking, and suddenly I collapsed.

When I regained consciousness, buckets of ice water were being poured over me. Apparently the Lieutenant wasn't enough of a savage to kill an unconscious man; it was only my fainting that saved my life. This incident was one of the many close calls that I experienced during my imprisonment by the Nazis. God was with me, however, and I cheated death for the first time.

It was the end of November 1944 when, after six weeks of marching, we arrived at the Austrian border. Of course we were never given a reason for the march and we had learned long before not to ask questions. Our Hungarian guards joyfully handed us over to the SS guards. We had no idea what was ahead of us but were fearful of what was to come. Our countrymen's farewell to us was: "It is time for you to get what you pigs deserve."

At the border, ninety of us, young men and women, were locked in a boxcar. The window was barred with plank wood and the door was locked from the outside. There was no place to sit and barely enough space to turn around. The overcrowding and insufficient air supply was suffocating, the stench of unwashed bodies nauseating.

There were two buckets in the car to be used for human waste. Most of us were teenagers and at first hesitated to relieve ourselves in front of others. It was painfully degrading, but as time passed we realized we had no alternative other than exposing ourselves to others. The buckets were emptied only once a day—at night—and their contents frequently overflowed during the day. As a result we sat in our own feces and urine for most of the day. The foul odor, hunger and thirst made us sick and caused some of us to faint. We were dehydrated and the few drops of water per day weren't enough to quench our thirst. Needless to say, the days and nights were filled with torment and misery.

Finally, after four agonizing days, our horrible journey came to a halt. Many of us were relieved and thought the worst of our misery was over. How wrong we were.

Arrival at the Death Camp

It was a gloomy autumn day; dark clouds were drifting across the sky as the cattle cars pulled into Camp 11, a sub-camp of Dachau located a few miles from the main camp. The compound was enclosed by high barbed wire, and surrounding its perimeter were watchtowers equipped with armed guards and blinding searchlights. Prisoners in striped uniforms and SS guards with revolvers in hand received us, shouting profanities as we were herded out of the cars: "Jew bastards! Rotten, filthy animals!"

The men and women were quickly separated and the women marched to their barracks, only a few yards from ours. Both were enclosed by barbed wire. Following the separation we were ordered to form a line, five people in each column, and the roll call began. The guards continued shouting, leaving us frozen with fear. Suddenly it began to rain and we were soon soaked and shivering in the chill of the night.

It was close to midnight when the roll call finally ended. We were shoved—drenched, hungry and exhausted—toward a large building where the guards ordered us to strip naked and leave all of our belongings outside.

"You will pick up your belongings when you come outside," the guards said. But it was only one of their many lies, for we never again saw our own clothing.

Once inside the building, the distribution of prison uniforms started. Our prisoner number was sewn on the jacket of each uniform, which was filthy and stained with the blood of a former owner who, no doubt, had been bludgeoned to death. Wooden clogs were distributed, which were clearly worn by other prisoners.

It was well past midnight when permission was finally given to go into our assigned barracks, poorly constructed wooden huts with no doors, only an open frame to walk through. There were no windows and no lights. Although it had a small stove in the center of the barrack, there was no firewood for heat. A mud floor was wet and ice cold.

Sixty of us were packed into the small living quarter that was hardly large enough for twenty men. We were squeezed together so tightly that it was impossible to turn from side to side. Eight of us shared one torn, filthy, lice-infested blanket; and as exhausted as we were, the pounding hunger pains and freezing temperature prevented us from sleeping.

__Life in the Death Camp__

It was four o'clock in the morning, still dark, when the shrill sound of whistles and the SS guards' barking voices ordered us out for roll call. Within seconds we lined up and stood shivering beneath the cold, starless sky. SS officers, with their ever-present German shepherds, walked up and down the rows and between the columns, inspecting our physical appearances. It was only a matter of luck who would survive the inspection; and those who didn't pass were beaten or shot to death.

I didn't notice at first when a tall SS officer in a spotless uniform stopped in front of me and asked for my number. My German was very poor and I couldn't quite understand his question; he asked me again. *"Ich sprechen nicht inhen Duetch,"* I said, "I don't speak to you in German." I meant to simply tell him I couldn't speak German, but he only heard the disrespectful phrase. His face turned red and like a wild beast he jumped on me and began beating me with his leather whip.

It was my first day in the camp and that episode made me realize the horror that was in store for all of us. Although I was in excruciating pain, what hurt me most was the humiliation and helplessness I felt at being unable to defend myself. As the monster beat me, I stood erect, taking his punches without a sound. I was too proud to cry. Following that incident, I memorized my prisoner number, 133057. Unlike the prisoners of Auschwitz, our numbers were not tattooed onto our skin. Nevertheless, my number was engraved in my mind and heart for eternity.

For the first three days in the camp, we received no food, only a cup of black liquid ironically called coffee. Following the roll calls there were a few minutes set aside to use the latrine, but due to the limited time, most of us had to wait until we arrived at the work site. From that first day, old-time prisoners told us, "Comrades, welcome to Hell on Earth." They warned us to take every opportunity to hide whenever and wherever we could. Otherwise, they said, we wouldn't last very long. I took their advice, but Imre, kind-hearted and naive, didn't listen to the older workers and believed the Nazis when they told us that we would be set free if we worked hard.

When we arrived at the camp I was in good health. I weighed 180 pounds and was optimistic about survival. The guards told us that if we worked hard we would receive good treatment. Many of my comrades believed their promise and worked even beyond the guards' expectations. They were beaten, tortured and slaughtered just the same and were among the first to die from exhaustion, starvation and sleep deprivation.

Hundreds of us were assigned to work in the Moll Commando, which was a large cement plant. The plant was a five-mile walk from the camp through a beautiful pine forest. We shared the temptation to escape and hide among the tall trees, but those who tried were gunned down before their dream came true.

As I dragged myself through the landscape, I recalled carefree, happy days that now only lived in my imagination. And for a few short moments I found myself in the forest of my childhood:

It is a beautiful, sunny day in May; the white and purple lilacs are in bloom, filling the air with their scent. Canaries and larks soar in the blue sky, their melodies echoing through the forest. My friend and I play hide and go seek among the majestic oaks, maples and poplars. Immense beauty and tranquility envelop us. Deer cross our path, their gentle eyes meeting our own. We always try to caress the deer, but we seldom succeed.

Squirrels play amidst colorful wildflowers and on tree branches, while woodpeckers feast on tree trunks.

The sun is warm and its golden rays shimmer upon the leaves, the ground and across the brook that runs through the forest. The water is clean and cold even in the heat of summer.

It is lunchtime; we sit by the water and eat our bread—it tastes delicious in this enchanting place of ours. There is an abundance of nuts, berries and edible greens in the forest and we nibble on the delicacies.

Time passes quickly, the sun is setting on the horizon, and the great Master of the universe paints the sky in orange, purple, and gold. It is time to go home, but there is always tomorrow; and as we say goodbye to each other, we promise to return again to our haven.

Suddenly, I feel a sharp blow on my back and a cold shiver runs through my body. Darkness envelopes me. My tomorrow disappears and only the painful moment remains.

Two of my comrades revived me, dragged me along, and somehow I found the strength to go on. By the time we arrived at the work site, our pain and exhaustion left us with only enough strength to lie down in our meager bunks. Nevertheless, we were forced to carry hundred-pound cement sacks on our backs. We hauled the sacks up a plank of wood, fifteen feet above the ground. Below us was a deep pool of wet cement and no rails to grasp should we veer too closely to the edge. Countless prisoners lost their balance under the heavy weight and fell into the cement pit. We watched in horror and with deep sorrow as our dear comrades tried to escape and desperately cried out for help. But we were not permitted to save them from their slow, agonizing death. I will never forget their screams, their sad, pleading eyes, and their arms reaching out to us as the cement swallowed them.

With the images of our comrades' fate, we were forced to go on. Our legs felt like rubber beneath us, our backs were aching and our heads were spinning from hunger. Yet, the guards screamed incessantly, "Go faster, faster, you lazy louses!" But our emaciated bodies could not keep up with the demand, and the savages beat many of my comrades to death.

During winter, the plank was covered with a sheet of ice and the casualties were overwhelming. Nevertheless, we worked from dawn until after dark, with only a ten-minute break for rest and to swallow the small cup of soup that was our "lunch." Around the work site there was lumber and piles of wood; and remembering a seasoned prisoner's advice, I hid behind them whenever the opportunity was present.

Every day, when our miserable journey back to the camp began, we were forty to fifty people short of the number of prisoners who began the day's work. At the end of the column, prisoners pulled two-wheeled carts with dead bodies—those killed during the day by torture, and those who died through accidents, exhaustion and starvation. When we returned to the camp, the dead were dumped into a mass grave and newly arrived prisoners took their places.

Those of us who survived the day received our "dinner," a small loaf of bread to share among twelve starving people. It was hardly enough to satisfy our constant hunger pains. Then, on the verge of collapse, we were forced to stand motionless for hours for the first evening roll call.

The Nazis were professionals when it came to torture. To achieve the desired effect, they used the most brutal and gruesome techniques imaginable, making our existence unbearable by various methods. During the day they forced us to slave from sunrise to sunset. At night they woke us eight-to-ten times for roll call regardless of the climate. We were frequently punished for unknown reasons and had to stay outside for the whole night in snowstorms, windstorms and sub-zero temperatures. Around us, fellow inmates fell, dead before they lay on the cold, wet ground. We often felt that they were the lucky ones, for they were free from abuse and suffering.

Every morning, as we ran outside for roll call, the guards greeted us with billy clubs, ready to beat our wasted bodies. Prisoners who couldn't endure the bestial treatment any longer gave up on life. They simply lay down and were then murdered.

The women in the camp had a variety of jobs; some worked in the kitchens and sewing rooms, others were housekeepers for the SS officers. I knew many of them from the cattle car that brought us to that living hell. When the veil of darkness fell upon the camp, I would sneak out from the barrack and crawl towards the fence of the women's barracks. Occasionally, one of the women threw crumbs of molded bread or rotten potato skins over the fence, priceless treasures for my brother and me.

To leave the barracks after roll call was a dangerous undertaking. The bright, rotating searchlights of the watchtower illuminated the campground. Nevertheless, I was willing to risk my life to keep my brother alive. Before dawn broke, I ran to the kitchen area where I knew that they were bringing out potato peels. The wagon containing the priceless treasure was watched closely by SS guards and camp police. With my eyes glued to the wagon, I waited anxiously for the right moment to snatch a handful of potato peels. When my mission was completed, I ran quickly and quietly away. The extra ration from the women's barrack and the wagons, paltry as they were, helped to sustain us.

One day as we were heading to work, I saw fellow prisoners in front of me grabbing bottles from a truck's bed. When I reached the mysterious truck, I too grabbed a bottle, hoping that it contained nourishment, such as soup; what I discovered was that the bottles contained water.

Suddenly, my fellow prisoners began throwing the bottles back into the truck. I looked up to see the reason for their action: two SS guards were running toward us. I tried to throw my bottle away, but the guards caught me stealing from their cart and beat me with their batons.

They asked for my prisoner number: "133057," I said. I was in pain and could hardly stand, but I was forced to work. All day, I prayed that the incident would be forgotten by the time we returned to the camp. I was terrified of what was in store for me.

Later, when the roll call began in the camp, the *Lager Fuhrer* came out from his villa and demanded that those who took the bottles from the wagon step forward. His request was met with silence—no one stepped forward. He became furious and said, "If none of you will confess to the crime, then your ration of bread will be withheld." We were starving and the few ounces of bread that was our dinner meant life. The *Lager Fuhrer* was losing his patience and began using his whip; still, no one confessed. Suddenly, I remembered what my father told me on that golden autumn day so long ago when I was seven. "My beloved son, always tell the truth no matter how painful it might be."

I stepped forward and was immediately seized by two SS guards. They took me into an empty room and told me to take off my prison uniform and bend down. The savages then beat me with their leather belts until I lost consciousness.

When I came to my senses, I found myself on a heap of snow tinted red with my blood. It was the extreme cold that stopped the bleeding and saved my wretched life. Two of my comrades picked me up and took me to the parade grounds for roll call. The counting started with searchlights focused on us.

Within a few weeks in the camp, our physical appearances changed drastically and we became mere shadows of our former selves. As we looked at each other we realized how rapidly our health was deteriorating: our eyes were those of frightened, hunted animals, and bones protruded beneath the flesh of our ashen faces. Our famished bodies were stooped; and the uniforms we wore—our only clothing—were filthy. Since we were unable to wash them, lice invaded our clothing and our bodies, and their bites soon erupted into open sores.

Our spirits were broken, our self-worth crushed. But one thing that our captors could not take away from us was our compassion for one another. For those of us who had a family member or a friend with him, that companion played an enormous role in survival. We all needed emotional and spiritual support and someone to encourage us to never give up on life no matter how miserable it was. My support was my brother; my feeling of responsibility for him gave my life purpose.

But there is a limit to the torture and starvation a human being can endure. There were prisoners who could not cope any longer with the brutal treatment at the hands of the Nazis; they chose death over a torturous life. They refused to get up and line up for roll call, knowing the consequences of their inaction. Their bullet-ridden, emaciated bodies were on display at the campground and all of us were forced to view our dear comrades. They were at peace; no more pain, no more grief. But our hearts were heavy with sorrow.

Winter at Camp II

With the arrival of winter our misery became unbearable; the only things occupying our minds were food, a place to lie down and heat to warm our frozen bones. About two or three hundred feet from the camp was a farmhouse with smoke escaping from its chimney. We all wished that we could sit by its fire if only for a few minutes; to eat a plateful of food to ease our constant, pounding hunger pains; to sleep in the comfort of such a house; and to be treated again like human beings. Once I, too, had a home; but now it lived only in my memory, where I returned often to the place that was so dear to me:

It is evening, the kitchen table is set for dinner, the kerosene lamp is lit, and we sit around the table enjoying the food and each other's company. We bask in the glow of the stove's purplish flame. Outside, the roaring wind taps on our windowpane, and snow begins to fall. Soon the ground is covered with a white blanket. The moonlight glistens on the snow and the stars glisten above.

Suddenly, the light goes out from the lamp, the fire dies in the fireplace and my family vanishes from view. I'm alone in the darkness, shivering and crying.

The SS guards enjoyed playing dirty tricks and we never knew from moment to moment if we would live or be slaughtered. It was on an early morning in January, a few minutes before work began, when a tall, elegantly dressed officer came out from his villa and greeted us with a friendly smile.

"You boys," he said, "are very lucky, for today will be warm and sunny." He began a conversation with us as if we were the best of friends, then quickly pulled out his revolver and began shooting, killing a dozen innocent people before the rest of us could run away.

We were shocked, unable to comprehend his vicious behavior. How could this seemingly friendly man suddenly turn into a wild beast? After that bloody massacre, the officer calmly walked away like someone who had done a productive day's work.

It was a cold January day—just before I started heading back from work—when a piece of wood on the ground caught my attention. I imagined a glowing fire in the small rusty stove that stood in the middle of our barracks. The stove never had the heat that this one piece of wood would create once it was lit.

I picked up the treasure and hid it under my uniform. Everything was going well until an SS guard noticed that I had something inside my jacket. He shouted, ordering me to stop. I quickly realized the extreme danger I was in and knew that severe punishment was in store for me.

I began to run and the SS guard started to run after me. But since he was overweight and middle-aged he couldn't catch me. He was furious and threw a heavy piece of wood at me. Strangely, I felt no pain, only something warm running down the back of my neck. When I touched my head my finger sank into a hole created by the impact.

Back in the camp, the infirmary doctor bandaged the wound with a piece of soiled paper and released me. Although the wound eventually healed, the scar is now an eternal reminder of the brutality of the Nazis.

One night there was a terrible blizzard; the temperature in the barracks must have been below zero. We tried in vain to keep each other warm, but our bodies were as cold as ice. I felt sick and shivered from the extreme cold. Yet when dawn arrived, I dragged myself outside for roll call. Sickness did not excuse us from work. The forest road leading to work was covered with freshly fallen snow and I had only one wish: to lie down and fall asleep forever. However, my sense of responsibility for my brother strengthened my resolve to live.

After our long march, we arrived at the work site— exhausted, famished, and dreading the long, hard day ahead. I was fully aware that unless I could find a hiding place I would not live through the day. There was a large pile of lumber a short distance from my workplace. That inviting hiding place drew my attention; and countless times I was tempted to crawl there; occasionally throughout the day I succeeded in slipping away into the lumber pile's safely.

From my hiding place I could see the guards watching some wretched prisoners who were carrying heavy cement sacks on their hunched backs. The ghost-like figures stopped just long enough to catch their breath, which was unacceptable to our captors. SS beasts turned on the pathetic prisoners and beat them to death. My heart ached for my dear comrades, but there was nothing I could do for them. I could only focus on my own survival. I trembled like a frightened, hunted animal trying desperately to be invisible to the vicious hunters. My ears strained to hear any footstep that might be the hunters' boots. The cold wet ground felt good against my feverish body, but I had to be on guard. For if the guards found me, I would be killed.

Time passed. How long I was hidden behind the woodpile, I did not know. However, I was roused by the barking voices of the SS guards, summoning the prisoners for roll call before returning to camp. Evening had fallen and the shadow of darkness settled over the forest as the procession of starved prisoners began the long journey out of Hell and back into Hell. At the end of the line there were flatbeds filled with the corpses of people who had died during the day. I left my hiding place and fell into line with my comrades.

We were barely able to stand by the time we returned to the camp. And then the endless roll call began once again. After hours of inspection we received our meager ration: a slice of bread and a cup of green liquid that was called soup. It was midnight before we were finally able to return to our barracks.

I was exhausted and feverish, and my feet felt like lead weights. My brother and a friend helped me to lie down. But the following morning I was simply too weak to get up. The barrack supervisor came to see me and realized that I needed medical attention. Since I couldn't walk, he had two inmates drag me through the snow-covered campground to the hospital.

The "hospital" was nothing more than a large barrack, with no heat, no beds, no sheets and no pillows. Dozens of us slept side by side on a plank of wood regardless of our medical condition. I was diagnosed with typhus but the doctor, who was also Jewish, had no proper medicine to treat his patients. He truly strove to ease our pain and suffering, but he only had Aspirin to give us. As a result, the days and nights were filled with the moaning, crying and praying of the deathly ill and dying. Many of the patients brought in never left the "hospital." It was either luck or destiny that allowed me to survive.

As my fever escalated I also became delusional and once again found myself drifting in and out of consciousness and calling for loved ones.

It is spring and my friends and I are roaming the blooming countryside. We pass fields and enchanting meadows covered with a rainbow of wild flowers. I run through the meadows amid the poppies, larkspur, daisies, mustard plants and cornflowers. I'm free as the wind, captivated by nature's beauty. I want to stay forever in this heavenly place.

Too soon, however, I regain consciousness, saddened to return to this hellish place.

I often tried to dissociate myself from my bleak, morgue-like surroundings and allow my imagination to soar, to return to my enchanting forest:

The fallen autumn leaves of golden-brown and reddish-orange form an exquisite tapestry on the ground. I sit under a tree listening to the withered, rustling leaves whisper farewell to the forest.

The harsh screaming of an SS officer jerks me back to my sad reality. I overhear the officer telling the good doctor to withhold from his patients the only medication at his disposal. Silence follows the officer's command, as he leaves the infirmary; and I know once again that our lives are in the hands of a vicious savage.

While my brother took every opportunity to visit me, he was not permitted inside the infirmary. Rather, he was forced to peek through a tiny opening in the infirmary wall. My heart ached for him for I knew he would be lost without me. Looking at those sad, hungry eyes staring at me I realized that I could not give up. I must survive, for my brother needed me.

It was winter and the inside the infirmary was as cold as outdoors. We nestled close to one another for warmth, our fevers ultimately blessings. Without that additional heat, many of us would surely have died. The only solace I found was in the dreams of my childhood:

It is a frosty night and the country road is enshrouded by freshly fallen snow. I'm heading home, enveloped in silent darkness. There is no sound around me; only the whistle of wind and the twinkling of stars keep me company. I yearn for the warmth of home and try to run but my legs feel heavy and every step requires tremendous effort.

Suddenly in the distance a faint light catches my attention. I gather all my strength to drag myself towards the illumination. As I approach the light source I see smoke escaping from it and I realize that it is a chimney. I am overwhelmed, I have returned home.

I peek through the kitchen window and feel my heart racing. A strange man is sitting at our table but I recognize the dishes, chairs, kerosene lamp and the cast iron stove, which I love. A woman busies herself by feeding the stove and preparing the evening meal while two unfamiliar little boys play on the dirt-covered floor. I begin to cry. Who are these strangers, I wonder, and where are my parents?

Imre's Passage

It was one of the coldest nights at the end of February. I had returned from the infirmary to my barrack. My bother was lying next to me, and in spite of the extreme cold, he was burning with fever. Although he never complained, I saw that he was in pain. I stayed up with him all night, but when it was time for roll call, he was too weak to get up.

I didn't want to leave him behind for I knew the severe punishment that came from being late for the count. He insisted, however, that I should go out and promised that he would follow within a few minutes. But when roll call started and I didn't see him, I became anxious. My first impulse was to run back to the barracks and carry him outside, but the viciousness with which the guards shouted their orders, and the brutality that followed, terrified me.

Finally the roll call came to a halt. When I returned to the barrack my world fell apart. On the cold, wet, mud floor was my precious brother. He looked at me with pleading eyes, tears streaming down his face, bruised and bloody from a beating by guards who were enraged by his failure to appear for roll call. I knelt beside him with a grieving heart and held him close as we both cried like children. I kissed his face and his trembling body.

I could see that he was in immense pain and tried to comfort him, but there was nothing that I could do to ease his suffering. Since he was shivering from his fever and wounds, I covered him with blankets. But no amount of blankets could keep him warm or ease his pain. My grief was overwhelming and I felt as if thousands of knives were piercing my heart.

"Dear God," I prayed, "have mercy on my beloved brother and take me instead of him." His emaciated, skeletal body was trembling and my heart was breaking as I helplessly watched him suffer.

Imre was barely able to speak but in a whisper he said, "I love you so much and want to be with you when the bell of freedom rings, but that isn't meant to be. I want you to be strong. Don't give up on life. And when this massacre comes to a halt, you must speak up on behalf of the innocent victims of hate. The world must learn about the horrendous crime that the Nazis have committed against humanity." I stroked and kissed his bruised face; and grieving, with tears in my eyes, I told him how much I needed him and how much I loved him.

He was in my arms when the door opened and two SS guards entered. They ordered me out of the barrack at once, but I refused. I didn't want to leave my dying brother in the hands of savages. Nevertheless, the beasts tore me away from him and I glanced one last time at Imre's beloved face. The guards were furious with me for lingering with my brother and disobeying their orders. "You filthy swine, you'd better hurry and get in line for work," they screamed. With no choice I left my brother's side and dragged myself through the frozen landscape to join my comrades.

The icy wind blew through my thin, frayed uniform. My bare feet were tucked into wooden clogs secured to my flesh with rusty wires, but the wires had long since broken the skin and caused infection. The frostbite, from which I suffered in my early childhood misadventure, reappeared with the first snowfall. Throughout my youth, my heels filled with a yellow fluid that Dr. Sandor drained. I didn't mind staying home from school because my mother showered me with love and affection. She made sure that the house was warm, the food tasty and plentiful, and the room cheerful.

On the day I was forced from Imre's side, both of my heels were inflamed, oozing with that familiar sticky, yellowish liquid. The pain was excruciating and I clenched my fists to avoid screaming. Despite my pain, it was my brother's torment that occupied me: the frail, wasted body coiled up to avoid the beast's merciless thrashing. I felt his agony; I saw his tears and my heart broke. I yearned to be with him to hold him and wipe away his tears, and I prayed to find him alive.

The day was endless, but darkness finally enveloped us and we headed back to the camp. I waited impatiently for the roll call to end and ran to the barrack. My eyes searched for my brother, but I couldn't find him. I ran to fellow prisoners, one after another, asking about Imre. Finally, a few eyewitnesses gave me the horrible news. They told me that shortly after our group left for work, the SS guards dragged my dying brother outside. They tied his hands behind his back with wire, and forced him into a tiny wire cage, shoeless and wearing only a thin striped jacket and pants. Sitting in a crouched position, my brother shivered in the snowstorm. With the icy wind beating on his skeletal body, my brother winced in pain. The savages put a potato in his mouth, depriving him from even expressing the basic human emotion of crying. My innocent kid brother froze to death alone.

He was only fifteen years old, a son devoted to his family and to God, an adored brother, and a beautiful human being. He paid the ultimate price for being a second late to roll call.

When the barbarians murdered my brother, a part of me died with him. I no longer had a reason to go on. Without him, life had no meaning and I would have died if not for a few good friends who cared for me and encouraged me to go on. I wanted to lie on our bunk and allow the SS guards to kill me; but my friends forced me to get up and go to roll call and to work. The hole in my life I filled with memories of Imre who often visited me in my dreams; I was so happy to see him.

We are children: he is three and I am six. It is a beautiful, sunny day in June and we are in Grandma's garden. The white and purple acacia trees are in bloom. The cherry tree is also in blossom and the apples and plums are ripe. We climb the trees and fill ourselves with the delicious fruit. The yard is alive with chickens, ducks and birds. Grandma's favorite cat, Shamu, is stretched out in the dusty yard, basking in golden sunshine. His curious green eyes follow the birds and flies, but he is too lazy to get up and chase them.

Suddenly, my bother falls from the tree and begins crying; I hug him and kiss him and he smiles up at me. Meanwhile, the sun begins to set on the horizon and invisible hands paint the sky orange and lavender. We say good-bye to our grandparents and head home for dinner.

Clouds begin to drift across the sky and a deep darkness surrounds us. I hold my brother's tiny hand in mine and he abruptly vanishes into the dark. I am devastated; I cry and call out to him: "Please come back to me, don't leave me. How can I tell our parents that I lost you?"

My weeping wakes my friends and they try to comfort me, but to no avail. I anxiously wait each night for my brother to visit and to spend a few precious moments with me.

The Liberating Troops

The days dragged on. It was the middle of April 1945 when rumors began to circulate in the camp about the Allied victory in Germany. When it became evident that American troops were only a few miles from the camp, the guards hurried to evacuate the compound.

While they wanted to destroy all of the evidence of their grisly, horrendous crimes, the SS guards were also determined to finish their genocide. They rounded up all of the prisoners and whipped us into a forced march to another camp: Allach. Those prisoners who were not physically able to withstand the torturous pace were shot dead and left along the roadside.

There was hardly enough time to settle down in what I later learned was a sub-camp of Dachau, when the long-awaited liberation day arrived: April 30, 1945. It was a splendid day, a day that I will cherish as long as I live.

There was no dramatic battle between the American troops and the SS once the liberators arrived. Just like the cowardly bullies they were, the Nazis fled once they saw that they could not overpower the Americans. The SS hurriedly exchanged their uniforms for civilian clothes (some, in various camps, for prison uniforms) and evacuated just ahead of the U.S. troops, leaving us prisoners behind. With their civilian disguises it was easy for the guards to escape into the surrounding forest and villages. Once the SS ran away the Americans opened the gate and our liberators marched in. Our hearts were filled with deep gratitude for the heroes who freed us. We kissed the hands of those brave soldiers and they tearfully embraced us, clearly pained by the sight of such human suffering.

Although we were alive, we looked more like dead men. Our deeply lined faces were the color of clay and only a thin layer of skin covered our skeletal bodies. From our original group of 240 people, only 18 of us survived that living hell. If freedom had been delayed by one or two weeks none of us would have survived. Seven months before, when we arrived at the first camp, I weighed 180 pounds, a perfect weight for a man of 5'11". At Liberation, I weighed only 70 pounds.

It was a bittersweet day. The shadow of death was all around. The foul odor of our dear comrades' decomposing remains filled the air, their skeletal bodies stacked in huge piles over the campground. Precious human beings, young men and young women in the prime of their lives, were brutally murdered, starved, tortured, worked and beaten to death. They represented so much suffering, pain, unfulfilled dreams and bitter tears. The world should never forget the deadly consequences of hate and of its innocent victims.

Our liberators comforted and reassured us, promising that no one would hurt us anymore. We were grateful for their sincere promise—and for the food we were denied for so long. However, it was not hunger that lured us from the camp, it was the sweet smell of freedom. I was weak and hardly able to stand, but determined to join a few friends to explore the world outside the concentration camp.

We roamed the green countryside, asking for food at homesteads and farms with whitewashed walls and red-tiled roofs. The German residents kindly fed us at their tables—

bacon, eggs, and bread—fearful perhaps of our liberators (who in fact treated them with kindness), certainly not fearful of us who were mere skeletons.

I often lagged behind on these forages for food and frequently had to stop and catch my breath. Even so, I would neither give up nor return to the camp. On Liberation Day I ate breakfast in half a dozen homes and by the end of the day I looked as if I had swallowed a watermelon. Terrible stomach pains were my reward for overeating, but I had no regrets.

However, food only gave me temporary physical relief; it could not fill the void left by my brother's brutal murder. Freedom without him was a lonely, sad event.

The Americans set up a temporary camp outside Allach, but we only went there to sleep; we wanted to be as far away as possible from any of the horrid SS camps. But roaming the countryside was a dangerous undertaking, since German soldiers were hiding in the surrounding forest. Some of them were still determined to fight the Allies and finish their genocide, despite what were clearly the end of the war and the danger of being caught by American troops. Night after night the shrill sound of their guns echoed through the now-American camp and we woke in fear of being recaptured.

As soon as we regained some of our strength, we began the search for our loved ones. After the Allied victory in Europe, many camps were established by the Allies to give temporary homes to the survivors of the Nazi death camps. These displaced persons' camps (DP camps) became places for us to live temporarily and find missing family members and friends.

I traveled from one DP camp to another hoping to find information about my parents, as well as family and friends from my birthplace or Miskolc. My journey took me to Feldafing, a small Bavarian town, and upon arrival I began my inquiries.

At first my search was in vain, but then I met Piri—a young girl from Miskolc and my friend Rudi's sister. Piri was also a survivor of the Nazis' crimes and, like me, was searching for people from her past.

Piri and I began to spend a great deal of time together and she joined me on my quest. We also took long walks in the countryside enthralled by the sun-kissed meadows and their colorful wildflowers. The surrounding pine forest was inviting and we sat for hours among the tall pines. We enjoyed the tranquility and the sound of the whispering trees, but we wondered how such splendor could exist in a country whose soil was soaked with the blood of millions of innocent people.

We often went sailing in an abandoned boat on the lovely Starnberger Sea, only a few miles from our DP camp. It was on one of those occasions that we almost lost our lives: We were the only people on the sea that day—our friend Alice, Piri and me. The sea was calm, the sky was blue and we were enjoying the serenity enveloping us. Suddenly, the sky turned dark. First, there was lightening and thunder, quickly followed by torrential ran. The boat began to rock and spin. Alice and I were excellent swimmers so Piri, who could not swim, felt secure with us. (It was only after we were safely on shore that I told her how terrified Alice and I were.)

Finally the storm diminished and we were out of danger, but Piri never again went sailing on the Starnberger Sea. (Soon after our adventure we found out that the last king of Bavaria, Ludwig, had drowned in that sea.) How fortunate we were, after our struggle under Nazi domination, to survive once again.

As the days passed I felt a tremendous urge to return to Hungary. I was very optimistic about my parents' survival for they were relatively young and healthy. But transportation in post-war Europe was extremely difficult due to the destroyed and badly damaged railroad tracks and trains. Nevertheless, in September 1945, I was able to get into a transport. Piri accompanied me to the railroad station, and when we said goodbye, neither of us knew if we would ever see each other again.

The train was jammed with passengers, the majority of whom were survivors like me returning to their homelands. Also like me, most were hoping to find family members.

As the train passed through cities and villages I recalled the journey I had taken the previous year, but my life was different now. Now I was free, traveling with a purpose, to my destination: home.

Hungary 1945

It took one week to reach Budapest. Evening had fallen by the time the train pulled into the station. Three hours later, I was on a connecting train to Miskolc. Despite the years I spent in the city that had been my second home, I felt like a stranger there. My first stop led me to an old friend's home where I received a warm welcome. Miklos and his family of five resided in a basement apartment and were very poor. Despite their poverty, they invited me to stay for as long as I pleased.

The news of my arrival traveled faster than the wind and I was met with great joy and surprise. Friends came to see me throughout the days and nights that followed. They brought with them food and clothing and offered emotional and spiritual support. It was a painful and often sad reunion for us—every one of us was a victim of the Nazis. Although we had survived, many parents and siblings, as well as extended families, were murdered. As a result, suicide rates were high among the survivors who couldn't cope with the reality of losing their loved ones.

I met with a few childhood friends from Szendro who had settled in Miskolc. The first thing I asked was news about my parents. There was an uncomfortable hesitation at first and I knew the answer would be devastating. Following a lengthy silence, some of my friends told me they were in the same transport and the same cattle car with my mother. When the convoy reached its destination—Auschwitz-Birkenau—the people were pulled from the cars and the miserable procession began. What followed was complete chaos. The brutal voices of the SS, with their vicious snarling dogs, terrified the children. The frightened Jews were then herded like cattle to the slaughterhouse.

At a huge square stood an elegantly dressed SS officer who decided who would live and who would die. His name was Dr. Josef Mengele, referred to as the Angel of Death. My friends told me that my mother was carrying one of her friend's twin children. The child in her arms meant she was automatically sentenced to the gas chamber.

My grief was overwhelming, but I still had hope of finding my father. But before I had digested the heartbreaking news about my mother, I was forced to confront another shock. I ran into George, a friend of my father's, who had been in the same regiment as he. They were on a freight train together, traveling through the city of Hatvan, Hungary, when there was an air raid. The railroad was the target of the attack. The train screeched to a stop and the passengers were ordered off the train.

My father refused to leave an injured comrade behind; and when the train was hit, he lost his life along with his friend. My father had died as he had lived, always helping others in need. I was devastated, the only survivor of my dearly beloved family.

A few days later, I visited the old synagogue. Only silence was there to greet me. A chill ran through my body as I stared at the decay and Nazi slogans scarring the walls. The windows were shattered and a thick layer of dust smothered the wooden benches and floor. I sat on a bench and tried to visualize how this once sacred place looked:

I hear the Cantor's beautiful voice filling the silence. The congregation prays softly and peace and love prevail in the house of the Lord. I see the smiling faces of children running and playing in the courtyard. The place is alive with their laughter.

But nothing remained of those children save the memories. The Nazis had forever silenced the children's laughter.

One day, as I walked down the streets of Miskolc I ran into one of my former comrades from the slave labor camp. I was thrilled to see him and asked him about his life in Hungary. A few minutes passed before he answered:

"Zoli, do you remember when we were in the slave labor camp?" he asked.

"How could I ever forget the humiliation and uncertainty of our future?" I said.

"And do you remember those Jewish girls we saw each morning as we were going out to work? How we envied them when we saw them sitting in comfortable carriages, going to work in the SS villas. They looked so well fed and content." His voice began to fill with tears.

"All of those beautiful young girls were brutally murdered," he said. His body began to tremble and tears ran down his grief-stricken face.

"When it was evident that the Russian troops were only a few days away from occupying Hungary, the girls were taken into the forest. They were given orders to dig a deep, large pit. Once their work was done they were forced to strip and stand at the edge of the pit. I'm sure by then the girls realized their fate but probably didn't have much time to think before they were gunned down.

"Right after the bloody massacre, they were covered with wet soil. Some of the victims were not even dead yet, and the ground shook as they tried in vain to claw their way out. Shortly after the grisly crime Russian forces occupied the country and the bodies were exhumed. My friend continued:

"I was among those who witnessed the horrid drama unfolding in front of us. It was a bestial act committed by human beings against their follow humans. As the victims were brought up one by one from their common grave my heart stopped for a moment, my head spun and I began to cry. I recognized my fiancé among the corpses, still wearing the necklace I had given to her for her birthday a year before."

As my friend told me the details of the grotesque crime, his body shook with the pain and sorrow of what he witnessed. I tried to comfort him, but I could find no words to ease his grieving heart.

Every place I went reminded me of the horror, torture and immense hate that the Hungarian Nazis still harbored for the Jews. My days and nights were filled with nightmares and painful memories of the bloody past. I felt in my heart and knew in my mind that I could never again be part of a country that had caused so much suffering and grief, one that claimed so many lives. There were other survivors who felt the same and we decided to leave Hungary.

A few of my friends got together, including Piri's brother Rudi whom I met while in Miskolc, and we planned the day and time for our journey. The night before our departure we met with several dear friends whom we were leaving behind. It was a tearful goodbye and none of us knew if our paths would ever cross again.

Szendro 1945

The day before we left Hungary I took an early morning train to my birthplace, Szendro. The countryside looked the same as the last time I saw it. I searched for familiar faces once I got to town, looking for friends from my lost childhood.

My father's family was happy to see me and tried its best to make me feel at home. They asked many questions about my ordeal in the death camp, which opened up fresh wounds. I had not really wanted to see my father's family because I felt disconnected from them, as a victim of Nazi brutality. But some of my former acquaintances persuaded me to visit them if only for a short while. The visit was strained and difficult; my father's family could never really understand what I went through. A few hours' visit with them and I was ready to return to Miskolc.

It was mid-day and my train back wasn't scheduled until 1:00. As I walked down the familiar dusty road, I felt a strong urge to visit the places that were once dear to me, especially the old fort where I had spent the best years of my childhood. I climbed the hill where the old fort stood and sat down by the large pit where my friends and I told ghost stories. My eyes filled with tears for the memories of those yesterdays.

I paid a visit to my enchanted forest where the fallen autumn leaves of orange, red, gold and brown covered the ground like an exquisite carpet. Everything looked as it did in my dreams during those horrid days in the camp. I sat among the withered, rustling leaves reminiscing about the carefree childhood days in my haven.

The sun began to set on the horizon, its purple-orange rays filtering through the almost-barren trees. The forest looked magical and I didn't want to part from it, but I had to catch the late afternoon train. I took one last glance at my childhood paradise and engraved the sight into my heart for eternity.

__Leaving Hungary__

It was dark when the train pulled into the station at Miskolc; my friends were waiting for me and we had a light supper before turning in for the night. However, we were too excited about our coming journey to get much sleep.

At three in the morning we dressed and headed toward the railroad station. We traveled very lightly—no suitcases, no backpacks—our only possessions the clothes on our backs, one kilo of bread and 20 grams of cheese. We had no money for tickets, but luckily were able to get onto the roof of the train.

The chilly autumn wind cut mercilessly into our faces and light clothing. As the train picked up speed and the wind increased, our situation became more precarious and we were certain we would be blown off the roof of the train. However, a gentle sunshine greeted us in Budapest. We were famished when we arrived and found a park bench to sit and divide the bread and cheese among the four of us.

It was midday, but where were we to go until our connecting train to Austria was scheduled to leave the following afternoon? We had an address in the city where survivors were fed and found shelter for the night. It was a Jewish organization called the "Joint" (American Joint Distribution Committee) where the staff welcomed us warmly and made us feel at home.

Following dinner we sat in the spacious living room and talked with other survivors. Every one of us had lost dear ones in the death camps.

Wallenberg and Budapest's Jews

While in Budapest we met with fellow Jews whose lives were saved by an extraordinary humanitarian, Raul Wallenberg. When murderous rage against the Jews was out of control, in the summer of 1944, a Swedish diplomat, Raul Wallenberg, came to Budapest.

By that time, the majority of Jews had been deported from the cities and towns to the infamous death camp, Auschwitz-Birkenau. Most of them were gassed. As soon as Wallenburg got to Budapest, he established safe houses for those who remained and whom he learned were condemned to die. A Swedish flag was proudly displayed outside the safe-house buildings, and he began negotiating with the high ranking German SS officers as well as the Hungarian Arrow-Cross members.

Wallenberg was a tireless, dedicated champion for justice and for human rights. Like a guardian angel watching over his frightened flock, he risked his life to save others. The savages, however, were determined to finish their genocide and almost succeeded.

During the night, when the city was enveloped by deep darkness, Hungarian thugs forced the Jews out of the safe houses. The miserable, defenseless souls were dragged to the riverbank, lined up, and were tied together. One person at the head of the human chain was shot; and as he or she fell into the river, the rest of the people on the chain were pulled into the icy water. Many Jews died in this way—with only one Nazi bullet spent.

When the Soviet army entered Budapest in January 1945, it was a bittersweet liberation day for the thousands of Jews whose lives were saved by that beautiful human being, for he was arrested by the Soviets and spirited away. The last anyone heard about Wallenberg was that he was transported to Siberia where it is assumed he died in a gulag. His memory, though, will live forever in the hearts and minds of those who cherish kindness, compassion and have the courage to fight against evil.

The Journey from Hungary to Germany

In Budapest, members of The Joint warned us about the great danger involved in crossing the border into Austria. Hungarian soldiers were patrolling the border and any escapees who were caught were tortured and thrown into prison. We were also warned about the land mines planted in the fields and were told about the victims of those mines. Nevertheless, and with few functioning railroads, we were determined to take the chance in our return to Feldafing.

As we waited for the train at the station we saw a few women handing out cigarettes. When we approached them and asked for a sample, we heard the hateful voice of one woman:

"Don't give any samples to those damned Jews. They should have all been killed in the death camps." Once again we were reminded of the extreme hate that our former countrymen held for us.

Finally the train pulled into the station and once more we climbed up to the roof, huddling together for warmth. The sun was setting and everything in sight was bathed in its orange and purple rays.

After a few hours, the train stopped by a large field and even though we didn't know where we were, we jumped off and began running. In the distance we glimpsed a human form. Overwhelmed and excited, we approached the stranger, who was a farmer dressed in blue overalls.

"Where are we?" we asked him.

"You are in Austria," he said.

"Do you know when the next train leaves for Vienna?"

He pointed to a small building in the distance, the train station, and told us: "The train leaves in twenty minutes; you'd better run if you hope to catch it."

We thanked him and ran as fast as we could; we were out of breath by the time we reached the station. There was not a single empty seat on the train, but even if there had been we had no tickets. We sneaked aboard and stood in the exterior stairwell, holding on to the rail with all our might. Luckily the wind had died and the weather had become milder.

It was already night by the time we got to Vienna and we set out to look for shelter for the night. Strolling down a darkened street, a sign for an inn caught our attention. We rang the bell and waited for the innkeeper to open the door. It took quite a while for him to appear; and when he finally did, he rudely asked what we wanted.

"We would like to have a room for the night," I told him.

The innkeeper was angry with us for disturbing his sleep.

"I have no vacancy," he said.

"Could you at least tell us where to find a room?" I asked desperately. He began to mellow a bit.

"I know a hotel where I'm sure there is a vacancy. Wait a few minutes and I will take you there." He returned quickly, in a friendly mood, and brought a bicycle with him. He told us to follow him on foot, which we did; and after about thirty minutes, he stepped off his bicycle in front of a large building, rang the bell and rode away. The gate opened and before us was a uniformed police officer. We quickly understood the innkeeper's dirty trick.

"What are you doing here?" asked the obviously surprised policeman. At first we were frozen with fear for we didn't know what to expect. But the policeman's reassuring manner gave us the courage to tell our story:

"We were brought here by an innkeeper who told us this place was a hotel," I explained.

"This is a police station," he answered, "and a jail. You can't sleep here . Even if I allowed you to sleep in one of the cells, the jail is currently filled up." He was a decent, well meaning man, but he couldn't help us. "Where do you come from and where are you going?" he asked us.

"We are survivors of the Nazi concentration camps, coming from Hungary and trying to return to the DP camp in Feldafing, Bavaria."

"I regret that I can't help you. But you may find some shelter over at the train station." We thanked him for his kindness and concern, and left.

On our way to the station we met a tall, unkempt and very drunk Russian soldier. One of my friends spoke some Russian and told the solider about our predicament.

"Don't worry," he grunted, "I will take care of you." As the five of us headed toward the station we began to feel uncomfortable with our new-found friend. I was especially unnerved by the way he kept his hand on his gun, swinging it as if he were ready to fire.

We finally reached the station, which was crowded with people. It took us only a few seconds to realize that we wouldn't find a place to sit; lying down somewhere was impossible. But our new companion had a plan. He saw a narrow dividing wall at one corner of the room and without any hesitation, tore down the plywood wall and provided us with a place of our own.

When dawn arrived our solider was nowhere to be seen. The station was still jammed with people; but through the crowd my eyes caught the sight of an immaculately dressed, clean-shaven solider coming our way. We could hardly believe that he was the same man who befriended us the previous night.

"I am a Lieutenant in the Russian army on a three-day drinking binge," he said with a wan smile. "When I go back to my regiment I will be placed in solitary confinement for two weeks." He embraced us and wished us good luck. We never saw him again.

We stayed in Vienna for two days before our journey to Feldafing continued. Although we still had no train tickets, we found a place to sit on the train; and I devised a plan that would convince the conductor that we were in our seats legitimately. My friends and I had disinfection cards with us that we received after liberation from the camps. The cards were written in English and luckily the conductor couldn't read them. They looked official and that was enough for the bored man.

Feldafing, Bavaria

From Vienna we traveled to Munich where we took a train to Feldafing. What a joyous reunion it was for me and for Piri, who I surprised with her brother's return!

In the DP camp, my six friends—including my future brother-in-law Rudi—shared a small basement room, without gas, electricity nor running water. The furniture consisted of two single beds and a hospital gurney shared among the six of us. We also had three chairs and a coffee table. We ate our meals in the communal kitchen, bathed in the communal bathhouse, and used the outhouse—all of which we shared with well-fed rats. But despite all the inconveniences we felt only gratitude, for we were free.

Freedom, we learned, is one of life's greatest gifts.

Zoli, far left, his mother, and his brother, Imre.
Szendro, Hungary 1939.

Zoli's uncle, grandmother, and his uncle's wife, 1939.

Zoli's uncle, front right, 1940

Zoli's father in a Hungarian uniform, forced labor camp, Ukrania, 1940.

Zoli's father, third from left, forced labor.1941

Zoli's mother and brother, Imre, 1942.

Zoli's grandfather, far right, with his co-workers, 1942.

Zoli's brother, on the right, with his friend, 1942

Zoli, 1943

Survivors in Allach, a sub-camp of Dachau, greet arriving
U.S. troops.
Region: Bavaria, Germany, April 30, 1945.
Watch tower in background.
Zoli was liberated from this camp.

Photograph: U.S. Holocaust Memorial Museum, courtesy of
National Archives. Photographer, Sidney Blau.

U.S. Army Corporal Larry Mutinsk puts cigarettes into the extended hands of newly liberated prisoners of Allach, a sub-camp of Dachau, Bavaria, Germany where Zoli was liberated. April 30, 1945.
U. S. Holocaust Memorial Museum, courtesy of National Archives.
Photographer: Arland B. Musser.

Zoli, center, at work as a barber in the Displaced Persons Camp, Feldafing, Germany, 1946.

Zoli's co-workers, Displaced Persons Camp, Feldafing Germany, 1946.

Zoli, 1947.

PIRI'S STORY

Preface

In 1941 Miskolc, Hungary, was home to about 10,000 Hungarian Jews. Beginning in 1942 the Hungarian labor service conscripted Miskolc's young Jewish men to work in forced-labor camps. By April of 1944 the last of the men left for labor camps. Hungarian gendarmes supervised the movement of the remaining Jews into ghettos. Between June 11 and June 14 of the same year, the Nazis deported almost all of the Jews of Miskolc, including 1,422 children. Most were transported to Auschwitz. Only 105 survived. And only twenty of the survivors were under the age of eighteen. Approximately 300 other Jews from Miskolc survived in labor camps.

In 1944, Piri was one of the millions of Jews rounded up by the Nazis and shipped to concentration camps. Her faith in God and her tenacity to hang on to a life that sometimes did not seem worth living, made it possible for her to be one of the very few Hungarians to survive the camps.

In Auschwitz, the most notorious camp of them all, Piri moved into the shadow of the "Angel of Death," Dr. Joseph Mengele. His directions determined life for Piri and her sister and death in the gas chamber for her mother, aunt, and numerous other relatives.

Piri faced life, witnessed cruel executions, and performed useless labor through the summer of 1944 in Plaszow Concentration Camp, which was run by German commandant Amon Goeth. In this testimony Piri recreates the beauty of life and the horror of Nazi inhumanity in startling detail. She brings the past and the present together in an emotional story of survival.

Dana J. Cordero

I am one of very few Holocaust survivors from Miskolc, Hungary, a city about 112 miles northeast of Budapest. Love and faith were the only wealth my family ever knew. These riches and a childhood of poverty enabled me to survive one of the darkest times in the history of the Jews. I left childhood behind in April of 1944 when I faced the horrors of Hitler's attempt to exterminate my people.

I didn't return to Miskolc until 1988. Since then I have audited classes at California Lutheran University where professors have encouraged me to write about my Holocaust experiences. At first I wrote for my family, so my children would know about my life. When I shared my story with CLU students, however, I realized the importance of young people understanding the significance of the Holocaust and believing it truly happened.

This testimony is the product of my experiences in the camp and my writing, interviews, and research into a time that is painful to remember, but which I can never forget. Indeed, the world must never forget.

The Occupation

German troops occupied Hungary on March 19, 1944. The miseries that followed in their footsteps changed my life forever and cast a haunting shadow on my memories and on the memories of those countless Jews who lived through the horrors of the Holocaust. We knew of Hitler's conquests in Europe, but reports of Allied victories gave us hope that the Nazi occupation would not spread into Hungary and the town of Miskolc, the home I had known for the nineteen years since my birth. There were rumors of destruction, torture, and death, but our immediate concern was survival.

I was born Piri Piroska Mendelovitz in Miskolc, Hungary on January 2, 1925 to a poor Jewish family. My father died when I was six, and my mother worried about feeding our family of four on the meager commission she made as a peddler, for her earnings often were not enough to buy fuel for the temperamental old stove that kept us warm. I worried about my mother when she traveled from village to village, from flea market to flea market, even in torrential rains and blinding snow.

I worried because Mother was a fragile woman, barely four feet, nine inches tall, weighing a mere ninety pounds. Her once-dark brown hair was sprinkled with gray, and by the time she was forty, her delicate face was engraved with wrinkles. The constant struggle for survival took its toll on her physical health, particularly weakening heart muscles due to malfunctioning valves. But her determination to provide for us conquered all obstacles. She never complained about her hardship, and there was no sacrifice too great when it came to her children. The time she was able to spend with us was limited, but it was enriched by love. We listened to her beautiful singing while we helped her cook the family meals, and cherished every precious hour spent with her.

Because we lacked money, I was forced to go to work following graduation from junior high school. Each morning as I walked to work, I encountered my former classmates going to high school. How I envied them: they were rich and were able to go to school, and I was too poor to continue my education; but I never let my mother see my tears of disappointment and pain.

At home our supper was often a small slice of bread, but I was thankful for the bit of jam Mother was able to spread on the bread. Even when there was no coal for the stove, I was grateful that I shared the narrow single bed with my mother and younger sister, Shari, for we kept each other warm. I was also safe in knowing that my brother, Rudi, whom we respected and trusted, was nearby on the couch.

Since my mother was often away for four or five days each week, our aunt Gissel, Mother's unmarried sister, frequently took care of us. She was a loving, wonderful aunt, but we preferred the company of our grandfather who lived in the same tenement. Even in his old age, Grandfather was a handsome man. His snow-white hair and long white beard reminded me of the paintings I had seen of Moses. His deep blue eyes reflected wisdom, compassion, and love. He taught us to be proud of our heritage, to believe in God, and to have compassion for people regardless of their religion, race, or ethnic background.

I sat by Grandfather's side for hours listening to enchanting stories from the Bible, lessons from the Talmud, and accounts of his life in Hungary. All of these tales, accompanied by his words of wisdom, gave the family strength when the future seemed hopeless.

"The bleak, gloomy days will pass," he said, "and the sun will shine on us." His words still echo through the years. Grandfather was right. We were poor, but the strength of our love for each other helped us keep a brighter future in mind. Love was indeed the nourishment and warmth that helped me survive the most difficult times of my life. The bleak and gloomy days did pass. I moved out of the shadows and today the sun shines on my life—because of my wonderful husband and precious children, and because of the lessons of life that Grandfather taught me.

We lived in the shadow of anti-Semitism before the German occupation, for Hungarian Nazis often made derogatory remarks about Jews. After the occupation, the already growing anti-Jewish decrees became pervasive. The Nazis were in complete control of our lives. Movement outside our home was restricted to daylight hours, and disregarding those curfews could mean death; many Jews who ignored the Nazi regulations paid the penalty.

Soon after the occupation, a proclamation was issued that all Jews must wear a canary yellow Star of David on their outer clothing. The Nazis claimed that it was a method of identification, but the purpose of identification soon became clear; the yellow star marked Jews as fair game for cruel treatment. We were easy prey. For example, we had to stand in line for hours to get our rationed food. When the clerks saw that we were Jews, they lied to us and said they were sold out of the items we needed.

This cruelty was not only delivered by the Germans. Many Hungarians were Nazi sympathizers who joined the fascist Arrow Cross, the Hungarian Nazi party. Arrow Cross members hated Jews. Their power over us reinforced their feelings of superiority. They could do anything they wished to Jews—even murder—for Jewish life, in their eyes, had no value. Taking the life of a Jew was an achievement, not a crime.

Our family became one of the many victims of their "achievements." One evening when my brother walked in the door, I saw tears in his eyes. Rudi hung his head as he told me how a group of young Nazis had jumped him on his way home from work. These youths were not strangers. They were Hungarians who had grown up in our town, gone to the same schools, and walked on the same streets as our family. He described how the boys attacked and beat him, then stuffed his mouth with horse manure. Rudi said he was all right, but I made him sit on the couch while I cleansed his wounds with a soft rag and cool water. I did what I could to ease his pain and care for his wounds, but nothing could wash away the humiliation of his experience.

Incidents like this one were everyday occurrences in Miskolc. Not one Jew was safe on the streets, regardless of age, sex, or status. Grandfather knew this, but he continued to go to the synagogue until the Nazis closed it. One Friday morning some friends brought him home after finding him unconscious in the street. Four young Arrow Cross members had ambushed him. The thugs had thrown him in the mud, torn out handfuls of his lovely white beard, and kicked him unconscious. People watched the brutal attack, but no one tried to rescue him. Even after this attack, he reminded us not to judge others because God would be their judge in the end. I often wondered how he could continue to respect his fellow man when people treated him so brutally.

The terror continued. Shortly after the Nazi occupation Jewish businesses were closed and Jewish peddlers were forbidden to sell merchandise at the flea markets where my mother had made our living. She was desperate. No income meant no food, no fuel, and no kerosene in the lamp. A compassionate Christian neighbor, Mrs. Stemlitz, understood our predicament and helped us: whenever a flea market was held nearby, she took my sister to sell the shirts and underwear my mother made. Because of the kindness of this woman, we were able to survive.

After the Nazi occupation, Jewish leadership confirmed the rumors that we would be relocated. When we heard that Hungarian Nazi authorities were confiscating all valuables from Jews, we gathered together our few precious belongings: a few family photographs, a necklace Father had given Mother, and Mother's wedding ring. They had little monetary value, but were precious to our family. Mrs. Layos, the owner of the fur salon where I worked, offered to keep them safe for us. When I handed her those mementos that morning, I had no idea they would be all the material possessions left of my life in Hungary.

One Monday afternoon in April, I came home from work to see my mother, her sad green eyes brimming with tears. As I put my arms around her and looked over her shoulder, I saw a half-filled suitcase on the table. I realized then why she was crying: our time for relocation was here. I told her I loved her, but she continued to cry bitterly. I had seen this kind of grief on her face before whenever we visited my father's grave. Mother's warm tears would fall on the cold stone, wetting the delicate cherry blossoms that partially covered the inscription, "Phillip

Mendelovits." I would stand in the shade of the cherry tree, the fragrance of wild lilacs floating in the air, crying at the sight of my mother's grief. My memories of Father are cloudy, but my Mother's anguish is impressed in my heart forever.

The half-filled suitcase remained on the table. Relocation: a cold, mechanical word that I would come to learn meant starvation, torture, and death. On that day, however, I only wondered with naivete how I could relocate my life and a home I had lived in since my birth. I did not realize then that the ultimate relocation was deportation and extermination of nearly all of my family.

We packed our few belongings for the journey to the ghetto. Authorities allowed us to take only what we could carry; but we did not have much. The few pieces of worn-out furniture we left behind had little value. Who wanted a shaky wooden table and chairs, a couch with springs jutting out of its worn fabric, and a single bed stuffed with straw? Even my mother's sewing machine that sat in the corner of the kitchen was old and rusted.

My sixteen-year-old sister, Shari, brought a cardboard box filled with pots, pans, and a few chipped clay dishes from the kitchen. She helped me pack a few pieces of clothing into the suitcase and closed the lid. Then, in the middle of our embrace, there was a pounding at the door. Six Hungarian gendarmes with revolvers burst in and ordered us out. They even refused to give us time to close the window or door.

I wished Rudi was with us but, at the same time, hoped that he was somewhere safe. He was twenty when the Hungarian Labor Service sent him, and most of the other young Jewish men in town, to forced labor camps a year earlier. It was the first year we were not together on our birthdays, which are all in January.

Grandfather came to our door, and I noticed tears glistening in his eyes as the gendarmes pushed all of us toward the road. I took one last glance at the shack that was our home. It was one of four dwellings in a single-level building with a dusty, unpaved yard. I could see the top of the white and purple acacia trees that bloomed near the Protestant cemetery bordering the back of our home. That cemetery held many childhood memories: Shari and I used to play hide-and-seek there. We looked forward to All Saints' Day in November, when families put flowers on the graves of their loved ones. At dusk, when the people had gone, Shari and I scampered among the graves, busily accomplishing our task. Some graves had elaborate floral arrangements and others had none, so we took a few flowers from each heavily decorated grave and put them on neglected ones until every grave had flowers. We never thought of it as stealing, but simply as sharing. After all, Grandfather had taught us to share with others.

While I thought about sharing those graveside flowers, the neighbors who we thought were friends had greed on their minds. They rushed into our home after we were forced out and took the meager belongings we left behind.

The sun was setting in a crimson-purple sky as Grandfather, Mother, Shari, and I joined hands and fell in step with other Jewish families moving down the road. The crowd grew as the gendarmes roughly shoved one family after another into the moving mass of Miskolc's Jews. I carried a suitcase, but my most valuable possession was in my heart. The childhood chapter of my life was closing, but my memories of a loving family would always be there.

On my first return to Miskolc, in 1988, I visited both my neighborhood and my father's grave. I remembered the day we left our home and saw, through the years, the long procession of Jews, the dust kicked up by the gendarmes' boots, and the dazzling colors of the countryside: red poppies, blue cornflowers, and yellow daisies filled the meadows as we passed. I wanted to pick a bunch of wildflowers for my mother, but if I had stopped I would have been shot. Death was already around me. But spring was in the air. I saw the rebirth of life everywhere . . . except in the eyes of Miskolc's Jews.

In 1988 I stood again in the shade of the cherry tree. It was then that I truly understood my mother's grief. She cried at my father's grave because she missed him and loved him. And she cried as she packed in 1944 for her beloved children's futures. Life continued, despite the shadows. I realized on my return that some things never change. There will always be people with hatred in their hearts. Greed, jealousy, and envy, will always be part of life, but love and compassion will always prevail. The sun will always shine, and the moon and the stars will always light up the sky at night.

Like the cherry tree, I have seen winter and experienced the dark and cold. The Holocaust was my winter, but I have also seen spring. My husband and children have brought beauty and sunshine into my life, and I thank God for His blessing and pray no one will ever see a winter like the Holocaust again.

A Fallen Angel

In the spring of 1944 my dark journey to the ghetto began. I was physically exhausted, emotionally drained, and frightened, but my legs carried me along behind the sad and desperate crowd. As I walked, it became more difficult to control my tears; I saw toddlers in their mothers' arms, looking over their shoulders, crying and pleading to go home. But home was no more; it was only a memory.

Laborers, scholars, businessmen, pregnant women, children, the elderly—all marched side by side with their lives in suitcases, backpacks, and boxes. The gendarmes herded us down the road like cattle, and we passed a two-story brothel on the outskirts of town. The red, pink, and purple geraniums that blossomed along its balcony would bloom until autumn. Would I see those blossoms again, I wondered?

The brothel reminded me of the year I graduated from junior high school at the age of fifteen and became an apprentice in a furrier's salon. I disliked my vocation from the very beginning, but it promised (so I was told) a decent future, even though as an apprentice I didn't yet receive a salary.

Mrs. Layos, my employer, was a widow in her late fifties. She was a big woman, six feet tall, with flaming red hair and piercing dark brown eyes—a shrewd businesswoman with

95

a hot temper and a sharp tongue. She had two sons, Arpad and Atti. Arpad, the older, was a science professor in a small college. He was only thirty-five, but he looked fifty—a timid, sickly-looking, quiet man with a keen interest in politics. Atti, the younger son, was in his late twenties and was the co-owner of the shop. Atti was an easygoing, friendly fellow with a great passion for women. He had a love affair with a prostitute from a nearby brothel. Erica was a gorgeous twenty-year-old girl with long golden hair and almond-shaped, hazel eyes. Her face was like alabaster, her teeth like a string of pearls. She was five-foot-five inches tall with a stunning figure. Erica loved expensive presents, especially furs, jewelry, and money.

Many times when Atti was short of cash, I took a fur coat or jacket to the pawnbroker to get a few dollars. I served as an intermediary between the lovers and became a frequent visitor to the brothel. Atti trusted me with his deepest secrets, and I never betrayed him. I became familiar with life in the brothel, and the girls treated me with love and respect. They always gave me delicacies, such as chocolates, figs, cookies, and oranges. It isn't surprising that I was anxious to be sent there.

The brothel was in a two-story brick building, much like the one we passed, with a white wrought-iron fence and gate. Customers came from a variety of backgrounds, ranging from professional men to businessmen to craftsmen. The majority of them were single or widowed. Young, old, and lonely men frequented the bordello. The music, the glitter, and the liquor created a festive atmosphere. For a few hours, worries, troubles, and the pressures of daily life were left behind.

I often wondered what happened to these women when they lost their charm, youth, and beauty. Indeed, the life they led changed their physical appearances quickly. Dark lines appeared under their eyes before they reached thirty-five, and sadness replaced their former sparkle.

I had heard that, when they were no longer profitable to the madam, they were turned out of the brothel. Most of these "ladies of the night" then found themselves on dimly lit street corners and in dark allies where they tried (often in vain) to sell their wasted, undernourished bodies.

I heard too that Erica suffered the same fate when, at the age of twenty-four, she became ill with tuberculoses and was dismissed from the brothel. Within a few months her life's savings were gone and she began to roam the city streets. Hunger is a powerful force that conquers pride and dignity. For lack of money, she searched the garbage cans for discarded food and slept under the open sky. Occasionally, she found refuge in abandoned, rat-infested buildings where she competed with the rodents for morsels of food. The harsh elements and lack of proper nutrition took their toll on her. Her condition rapidly deteriorated, and when she collapsed on the street she was taken to a hospital.

I visited her in the hospital and was deeply saddened by what I saw. Her frail body lay quietly under the coarse, torn, faded blanket. The once-alabaster face was pale and sunken, she was burning with fever, and her golden hair was tangled and soaked with perspiration.

It was a splendid day in the middle of October. The last rays of the setting sun illuminated the charity ward's gray walls and danced upon the cold cement floor. Erica, with the help of an aide, dragged herself to the half-open window to behold the splendor of nature. Outside, the withered autumn leaves began to fall. The ground was covered with a mass of orange, red, gold, and brown leaves, and she could hear their moaning, rustling sounds. Her eyes were filled with tears as she recalled the days long, long, ago when, as a child, she played among the fallen leaves.

The glorious sunset turned into a starry night. From her bed, Erica saw the silver moon smiling down on her. Suddenly, the fragile body was shaken by a violent cough. Her breathing became labored and shallow. The gentle heart was giving up, and soon it ceased to beat. Her journey on earth came to an end when the stars faded from the sky.

The Ghetto

The brutality we had known immediately after the occupation was nothing compared to the treatment we were subjected to on the way to the ghetto. The gendarmes took delight in tormenting us. "Dirty pigs," they called us, and whipped us with the butts of their rifles. Anyone who stopped for even a moment was beaten brutally. Families looked on in shock, but were not allowed to stop or help their loved ones.

At last, the crowd halted at a building where the guards separated the men from the women and directed us into rooms where we were searched. The Nazis were sure that we were all hiding something of value. One of the gendarmes supervised the prostitutes who searched my mother, Shari, and me. He smiled sadistically as the women probed every possible private area for some kind of hidden wealth—wealth they did not find.

When the humiliation was over we continued to march to the area designated as the ghetto where my cousin Mariska and her family lived in a poverty-stricken, neglected section of Miskolc. Our extended family of twenty-five moved into the small, sparsely furnished one-bedroom apartment. At least three or four families occupied each dwelling, and those who didn't have relatives in that part of town were assigned living quarters with other families.

The four older members of our extended family shared the one double bed, while the rest of us slept on the cement floor. Meals were prepared on the table near a rusted stove, but there wasn't much to prepare. If we were lucky there were enough potatoes or noodles for everyone. Most of us sat on the floor to eat because there were only two chairs in the apartment; and most of the time we all went to bed hungry. In the bedroom where we slept there wasn't much need for the dresser. We only owned what fit into the one suitcase we had brought.

We were not allowed outside the ghetto, which was guarded day and night by Hungarian gendarmes. A handful of Jews who were designated to shop for the ghetto inhabitants were escorted to the marketplace, where peasants from the surrounding area sold fruit, vegetables, and chickens. Of course, those unfortunate people who had little or no money were unable to buy enough food to sustain themselves and their families.

I stood at the window of our ghetto apartment, tired, hungry, yearning for relief from the oppressive heat and powerful stench of unwashed bodies. But there was no relief. An inadequate water supply and overcrowding created unsanitary conditions. In addition, the window overlooked an open sewer from which vicious rats came up during the night and scavenged through our scanty food supply.

I could bear the lack of food since our family was accustomed to getting by on very little, but I would have given anything for the luxury of a bath. I would not have cared how far I had to carry the buckets of water. At home we had to carry water from a pump a mile away, but we could have as much as we needed. In the ghetto we were lucky if all twenty-five of us had one bucket of water a day.

I spent much of my time daydreaming during those weeks. There was little else to do, particularly as conditions grew worse in the ghetto. I longed more and more to be at home, despite its imperfections, even despite the offensive smell of the outhouse during hot summer months. After school we often played hide-and-seek or soccer with a rag ball with other neighborhood children. Sometimes, if I felt like being alone, I went to the meadow, to its delicate scent of flowers. I wove beautiful dreams there, dreams of a world free of pain, sickness, and poverty. From spring to autumn, wildflowers of every color in the rainbow bloomed; and I sat at the end of that rainbow. I watched butterflies chase each other from petal to petal, and listened to the enchanting melodies of larks and robins drifting on a gentle breeze; and I dreamed of a life as carefree as it was in that meadow.

It was night and a child's crying brought me back to the harshness of reality. My cousin Mariska's two-year-old daughter, Susie, was hungry; but how could we explain to a two-year-old child that there was no more food? I walked outside to get away from the cries and confusion. Once I felt free and happy outdoors, looking up at the black velvet sky with its dazzling brilliant stars. Now, guards surrounded the ghetto and evidence of our confinement was everywhere, tainting nature's serenity.

We were trapped inside. Non-Jews could not legally enter the ghetto, but a few friends slipped inside in an effort to help. My former employer, Mrs. Layos, brought us food several times. One day, just as I was thinking about her, I heard someone call my name. I looked around and saw Mrs. Layos near the corner of the building.

"Piri," she said, "I have such good news for you. My neighbors, the Gyetvais,' have a country estate at Disznoshorvat. They need people to work in their fields. I have made arrangements for you, your mother, and your sister to be released from the ghetto to work there."

"Oh, Mrs. Layos," I said, "are you sure?" Can we really leave from here? But how will we. . . ?"

"Don't you worry; the guards will come for you. I don't know how long they will let you work there, but it will be much better than here. The Gyetvais' will treat you kindly and feed you well.

I wanted to hug her, so grateful was I, but I knew that if she stayed by the fence too long she would arouse the guards' attention; so we said goodbye and I ran to tell Mother the good news. I remembered the Gyetvais family from the many trips I made to my employer's house. I would often run errands for Mrs. Layos and occasionally I would run into the Gyetvais' twenty-two-year-old son, Peter. I had a crush on him the first time I saw him, but I didn't think he noticed me. Peter was a lieutenant in the Hungarian Army, and my idea of Prince Charming. He was of medium height and build, and his wavy chestnut hair was always perfectly in place.

The next day, gendarmes escorted the three of us to the Gyetvais' estate. Our quarters were in the barn, but it was clean and the space was adequate. We worked hard there, and it was good to have our stomachs full again.

Peter was home on leave while we were there and kept asking that I be allowed to stay behind when my mother and sister went to work in the fields. I was a naïve nineteen-year-old girl and flattered by his attention, but my mother suspected that the young lieutenant wanted more than my company, and she insisted that I go with them to the fields. Fortunately, Peter, who could have ordered me to stay behind, didn't use force.

We lived and worked on the estate for about three weeks when our good fortunate ended. The gendarmes took us back to the ghetto where the days and weeks dragged on.

Ghetto life was especially hard on the very young and the very old. Children were hungry and cried constantly, and everyone was frightened and slept less and less. Tragically, many people couldn't cope with the humiliation and deprivation, and they committed suicide.

Rumors of another relocation brought renewed anxiety. We knew we would be moving again, but we didn't know where or when. We tried to encourage each other, to tell each other that the next move would be to a better place, but in our hearts we knew the situation would only get worse. Eventually, the movement into the shadows did worsen. It started with the familiar sound of marching boots, and before we knew what was happening, men and women were screaming, children were crying, and Hungarian gendarmes were brutally forcing Jews out of the ghetto.

The Brick Factory

We looked like a defeated army with our heads bowed and our feet dragging as though they were made of lead. We were tired and weak, broken in spirit and heart as we straggled along the dusty, familiar road. The Hungarian gendarmes herded us like cattle and kicked us repeatedly with their heavy boots; they were clearly enjoying their unlimited power over us.

We walked about six kilometers to Diosgyor, a small community of about 5,000 people most of whom worked in the local brick factory. My family was among the thousands of Jews who were being gathered in the courtyard of that factory. The day before we had a meager roof over our heads, but that was yesterday. Now we were homeless. We slept beneath the cold, open sky, deprived of privacy and human dignity while vicious murderers guarded us. The nights were filled with the cries and screams of victims who were beaten and sexually abused. There was no pity, no mercy, no assistance from the Hungarian government, nor did anyone seem to care what was happening to us.

Families prepared food in huge kettles and cooked over open fires. We contributed to the scanty food supply what we had and shared our meals with those who were hungry. A crust of bread could mean life to a child, but often it wasn't enough, and many children fell gravely ill and died.

One morning, when I woke from a troubled sleep, I looked at my grandfather and barely recognized him. Even at his advanced age of seventy-two, he was a handsome man, a man whose knowledge of the Talmud and the Torah, politics, science, history, and medicine earned him the respect of all who knew him.

But the grandfather who sat before me was a broken man. His warm, bright eyes were filled with tears. During the night, the gendarmes had chopped off his beautiful white hair and beard, burned his prayer book, and ripped his prayer shawl, violating the sacredness of the Orthodox Judaism in which my grandfather so devoutly believed.

Seeing my grandfather so humiliated made my heart ache. Without his white beard he looked naked. I wanted to do something about this inhuman treatment, but I stood defenseless against the cruel Nazi beasts. The only time I had seen such anguish on Grandfather's face was when his son, my father, died at the young age of thirty-three.

As I looked past grandfather, across the factory yard, the dirty red bricks reminded me of the cold red buildings of the hospital where Mother had taken me to visit my father shortly before he died. Father had come home from work on a hot July day with a severe headache and a high fever. Nausea, and vomiting followed. Mother took him to the hospital where the doctors diagnosed his illness as sunstroke. But his condition deteriorated rapidly, and when it was too late to save him the doctors realized he had meningitis.

Father had a premonition that he was on his deathbed, and he asked to be taken home from the hospital. A day after he came home, he was gone. It was a Friday afternoon, and following Jewish tradition his body was kept at home until burial on Sunday. For two days and two nights, Grandfather sat up guarding his son's lifeless body.

It was difficult for us as young children to accept Father's death while his body was still at home. He was gone, but his smile, his love, and his spirit surrounded us.

On the morning of the funeral, Grandfather prepared his cherished son for the eternal journey. Tears streamed down his face as he washed Father's wasted body and lovingly wrapped it in a coarse, white shroud. He placed the traditional gold-threaded, white shawl over Father's shoulders, kissed his son goodbye, and prayed for God to receive his soul with love.

My memory faded and the bricks came back into focus, but it wasn't the hospital I saw in front of me and I was no longer a child. Grandfather had the same grief-stricken look on his face as he did when his son died; but whose death was he now mourning? In less than a week I would know.

Grandfather became weaker, but his strong belief in God was never shaken. Even in the shadow of death he believed in honesty, justice, and human rights. But what kind of honesty, justice, and human rights were these? What kind of humans were these Nazis who were taking over Europe and treating us as if we weren't even human? Grandfather and Mother had planted the seeds of love in my heart and mind, teaching me to believe and trust in God. And I did believe in God, but it became more and more difficult to put my trust in people. I knew that only God could get me through the journey ahead.

Today when I see bricks, I remember the hospital and Father's death, and I see Grandfather's bruised and bleeding face and feel the anguish of a journey that began in a brickyard.

Within the first week of June, our stay at the brick factory ended. Hungarian Nazis waved whips and truncheons, screaming as they herded us away from the brickyard. "Move faster, you filthy pigs," they shouted. We walked as fast as we could but some of the elderly and sick people couldn't keep up, and those who lagged behind were shot to death.

It was a scorching hot day, and I was soaked with perspiration. I was only a tiny drop in the wave of humanity that rolled seven miles down a dusty, rutted road. Local residents with curious, emotionless eyes stood in their doorways watching the caravan of refugees, but no one made a move to help us. They didn't even offer us a drop of water. Cows or horses would have been given water, but not us—we were Jews. The Hungarian and German Nazis didn't believe that we were human; we didn't even have the rights that animals enjoy.

Finally, after hours of exhaustive marching, we arrived at a station where a convoy of cattle cars was waiting for us. When I saw those cars, I knew our journey would take us farther away from home than I had ever been; and I remembered my uncle who had offered more than once to bring me to his home in the United States. But America was so far from home, and I didn't want to leave my family. Now as a family, we would all be far from home; but at least we would be together, or so I thought.

The Hungarian gendarmes were delighted to hand us over to the German SS when we got to the train station. It took only a few moments before the SS guards began shouting their commands and shoving us into the cattle cars. It was then that Grandfather blessed us, and told us never to lose faith in God.

As we tried to hug each other, Grandfather was pulled away, and we were shoved in opposite directions. I scarcely recall how I climbed into the car; I just remember the sound of the heavy door sliding shut and the bolt locking it into place from the outside. That was the last time I saw my grandfather. I prayed for God to take care of him; only He could help any of us now.

My mother, Aunt Gisele, Shari, and I were jammed into the car with about ninety other men, women and children. There was hardly any room to stand and only the elderly and sick were allowed to sit where there was room. Soon we heard the rhythmic clanking of the train's wheels, and our unknown journey began.

A lone square window was barred with planks of wood, preventing escape and keeping fresh air from circulating in the car. The heat was stifling. I was surrounded by acrid bodies all dripping with perspiration. Two pails stood in a corner to be used for human waste. At first, everyone hesitated to use them, for it was degrading to relieve oneself in public; but we soon realized that there was no alternative. Often the bucket was too full, and its contents overflowed. People sat in their own feces and urine, and the stench was unbearable.

The car was suffocatingly hot, but we were given only a few sips of water each day. People vomited and fainted. Children screamed relentlessly; they were hungry, thirsty, and tired. But as the hours and days dragged on, their voices lost strength, their cries turned into whimpers and soon the sound of their voices ceased altogether. The tiny, lifeless bodies were held protectively to their parents' hearts. Mothers went berserk watching their children suffer and die. I watched in disbelief the shocking crime that was committed against defenseless, innocent people and asked myself how, if God created the world in His own image, there was so much ugliness. There was never an answer.

Each night, the cattle train stopped for a short time, and the dead and dying were thrown from the train. We learned from eyewitnesses that our grandfather was among the dying, disposed of like garbage along the cold, wet, and lonely railroad track. I am sure to this day that he died with God's name on his lips.

As the days passed, the number of survivors declined. We were too tired, weak and hungry to care anymore and wished that the end would come. But our beloved mother embraced us and told us that we must be strong and never give up hope.

We Will Not Forget

Dedicated to my dear sister, Shari, whose unselfish love and devotion helped me survive the horrors of the Holocaust.

It was a rainstorm, a windy autumn night
Thunder shook the earth, lightning lit the sky
Far away from home in a concentration camp
My sister and I held each other's hand.

Covered up in rags, without shoes or hat
Standing motionless by a railroad track
Freezing and shivering, tears filling our eyes
Waiting for the train throughout the whole night. . . .

Thousands of prisoners stood in line with us
Crying silently and praying to God
The guards used their clubs and rifle butts
Innocent people were murdered in cold blood.

Their lifeless bodies fell on the cement
The vacant eyes seemed to be questioning heaven
Their blood flowed like a red river
And the Soul was drifting toward heaven.

By midmorning the freight train arrived
We were locked in cages like animals
Behind the closed doors my sister and I
Embraced each other and began to cry

Shari was just a child, but mature in age
She encouraged me to be strong and brave
"You will see," she told me, "soon we will be free,
But we must believe and not lose our faith."

She had kept me going and took care of me
Jeopardized her life by stealing food for me
With her gentle kiss she wiped away my tears
Without her loving care, the pain I couldn't bear.

Then one sunny day in May of '45
We were liberated with a new lease on life
But we swore to God, the world will not forget
Our six million martyrs who were tortured to death.

Piri Piroska Bodnar

Auschwitz-Birkenau

The screech of brakes replaced the clank of wheels on the track as the train slowed to a stop. I heard the familiar knock of the door bolt releasing and prayed we would get some fresh water or a crust of bread. I knew I couldn't make it through another sweltering day in that cattle car. I was weak from four days without food, water, or sleep.

When the door slid open I expected to see Nazi uniforms, but instead strange-looking creatures in striped shirts, black pants, and caps greeted us.

"Out, out, out—faster, faster, faster," they yelled as they swung truncheons left and right like robots; their movements were mechanical, drained of all emotion, and their faces expressionless. Later I learned that most of these men were Jewish prisoners themselves. They pulled us down from the cars and shoved us into the crowd.

The nightmare continued as we stumbled in the direction we were pushed. Choking, thick smoke covered the sky like a gray blanket. I tried to catch my breath, but my nostrils filled with a strange odor that I could not identify and I trembled with fear when I saw flames leaping from the tall chimneys that dominated the landscape. One of the prisoners in a striped uniform must have seen me look toward the chimneys, and said with blunt indifference, "Those are the ovens where people are cremated." But before I could question him, he was gone, and the crowd carried us toward the entrance of an immense compound surrounded by barbed wire. I couldn't believe all that I heard and saw. How could it be? What were the Nazis protecting with these fences?

I thought of the chicken wire Mother placed around her garden. She loved flowers, but when she planted petunias, pansies, and marigolds, the neighbors' chickens harvested the budding plants before they bloomed. Mother didn't give up, however. She protected her flowers from the chickens by surrounding the bed with chicken wire. When we got closer to the electrified barbed-wire fence, however, I realized that this wire didn't serve the same purpose: it wasn't there to protect us: rather, it was there to imprison us.

Inside the camp, row after row of barracks stretched as far as I could see. I was one of thousands moving through the gates. The arch above our heads read "Arbeit Macht Frei" (Work Makes One Free). But I soon learned that no amount of work would ever make us free in the eyes of the Nazis.

There was confusion, crying, and despair in those early moments when the SS guards started separating the men from the women. My mother, Aunt Gisele, Shari, and I managed to stay together, but many families were separated. Grief-stricken parents called to their children, but were not allowed to search for them. Toddlers stood petrified and lost in the chaos. Strangers picked them up and tried to comfort them. Those humanitarians didn't realize that they would pay with their lives for befriending a child, for anyone carrying a baby or holding the hand of a toddler was automatically sent to the gas chamber. It seemed like we were all being swallowed through hell's open gates.

SS guards with vicious dogs herded us into a large square where a tall, elegant SS officer stood. He had a clean-shaven face and wore an immaculate, tailored uniform with shining buttons. I will never forget the sadistic smile on the face of Dr. Joseph Mengele as he pointed his baton right and left. I learned that this self-proclaimed god was known as the "Angel of Death."

When it was our turn, we stood in front of him. "I am strong and will work very hard; please let me go with my children," Mother pleaded.

"You will see your children soon," he said as he pointed in the direction of the women who were carrying infants or holding the hands of toddlers. Mother and Aunt Gisele followed the crowd. One last glance, a tearful goodbye, and they were swept away. I never saw my mother again.

Shari and I hugged each other and began to cry. Mengele pointed in the other direction, a guard shoved us with his baton. I didn't understand then what "left" and "right" meant, but I realized soon enough which one was the road to death. My mother was sent in that direction and murdered in the gas chamber. If this was a dream, I wanted to wake up at home and see Mother in the corner of the kitchen at her sewing machine. I wanted to hear her sweet voice singing as she worked. But it was not to be. I was living a horrible nightmare.

Shari and I stumbled along following the crowd. We heard wheels grinding behind us and turned to see prisoners, guarded by SS officers, pulling a cart filled with babies and small children. The tiny terror-stricken victims trembled and screamed, and tears rolled down their dirt-smudged cheeks. We wanted to stop and comfort the lost and lonely orphans, but we were forced to continue walking. A few yards away we saw a huge roaring fire. Later, long-time prisoners told me that those babies and toddlers, whom we saw earlier, were thrown into the fire alive!

How could God allow this brutal slaughter? Where was God? Why were we here and why couldn't Mother stay with us? More questions and still no answers—only the certainty that it was a matter of time before Shari and I would meet the same fate as our mother.

We moved along blindly through the maze of horrors, fearful of what was next. When we came to a large building the guards told us to strip and leave all of our belongings outside. They shoved us naked into the building for showers. The water was scalding hot and burned our flesh like a rain of fire. The guards watched through peepholes and snickered as we cried out in pain.

After the shower, prisoners shaved our heads, armpits, and pubic area. We were then forced to run naked and wet to another building. There, clothing in all sizes was stacked in piles and distributed to us. No one asked what size we wore, or seemed to care whether or not the clothing fit us. Ultimately, the garments we were given were nothing more than dirty rags. Shoes were mismatched, each a different size. Women's shoes, men's shoes, wooden shoes, leather shoes—all were strewn together. (I was given a pair of wooden shoes that were far too big.) We received no socks, underwear, sweaters, nor jackets. We tried to trade the worn, ill-fitting clothing and shoes with each other, but we barely had time to cover our wet bodies when the guards shoved us out of the building.

I was dazed, but still holding Shari's hand; we were determined to stay together. As the crowd moved along, groups of women were shoved into barracks that were already filled with prisoners. I was glad when our turn came. I was exhausted and only wanted some sleep.

The wooden hut was damp, cold, and dark. There were no windows and no ventilation. I collapsed on the floor and closed my eyes. What a luxury was the little bed Mother, Shari, and I shared. How I wished for its straw mattress instead of the half-dried mud floor under my head.

In no more than five minutes a sharp whistle sounded and snarling voices ordered us out. The dreaded roll calls had begun. We had to stand motionless in the cold night to be counted and recounted, undoubtedly just to exhaust us emotionally and physically—to break our spirits. We were weak, hungry, and emotionally drained from our four-day journey. It was after midnight when the guards finally let us go back to the barracks. But before we could fall asleep the whistle blew again.

The cursed roll calls continued day and night, night and day. Ten or fifteen times a day we stood in the stifling heat with our lips blistered, our throats dry, and our tongues swollen, without a drop of water to quench our thirst.

SS officers walked down the rows of prisoners and randomly shot people who were standing quietly in line—simply for their own amusement. People who fainted because of fatigue, thirst, and starvation were also killed. We never knew from one moment to the next who would be the next victim. The SS took pride in killing Jews. The more Jews they killed the more their superiors seemed to acknowledge and respect them. Every day thousands died, not only from torture and murder, but also from exhaustion, malnutrition, and disease. I wondered how the guards could go home each night and become loving husbands and fathers after the atrocities they committed against us each day.

One night after roll call the whistle blew and we staggered out of the barracks..

"If you die, I don't want to live," Shari said as she grabbed my hand.

"If a guard shoots you, I will step out of line and also face death," I told her.

We decided that without each other we had no reason for living. Needing one another could have killed us, but it kept us alive.

The crematoria couldn't handle the heavy load of bodies from the gas chambers, so prisoners were forced to pull carts loaded with corpses and dump them into mass graves. The misery and the torture were too much for me to bear, and I could no longer hide my tears. I cried while the beasts weren't watching and I was proud of my tears because they showed that I still had feelings. And in spite of everything I had suffered I still believed in God and in the sanctity of life, even though I knew it was easier to die than to live.

At night, the rotating reflectors on the watchtowers were like monstrous eyes watching our every move. There was no way to escape the guards and their machine guns. Auschwitz-Birkenau was surrounded by electrified barbed wire, which was used frequently as a means for suicide. I saw many such heartbreaking instances in which prisoners could no longer cope with torture and starvation. Death was easy; but life for them was unbearable.

The victims ran to the electric fence with outstretched arms, tears on their pale, sunken faces. With hands clutching the deadly electric wires and glazed eyes facing the sky, they looked for eternal peace, freedom from despair and brutality. However, death on the electrified fence was not always to be, for the guards shot them before they could reach their destination. Even death on those poor souls' own terms was not of their choosing.

How could a normal world continue beyond the barbed wire? How could people nearby not see the savage behavior of our oppressors? Didn't they wonder about the chimneys that belched fire and poured ash on their town? The sun was hidden by a sky heavy with gray ashes, but beyond the barbed wire well-fed, well-dressed men and women walked by our camp each day on their way to work, as if all of it were normal.

We shared our dreams about the contents of their lunch boxes; and we talked about the lunches we would prepare if we were free. In the barracks our conversations were always about food. We exchanged recipes and described in great detail the preparation of our specialties, trying to outdo each other with the lavish gourmet creations of our minds. In reality, any one of us at any moment would gladly have given her life for an extra piece of bread or a portion of "grass soup."

There was widespread sexual abuse in the camp. The guards were free to choose and use any young girl as often and as long as they wished, despite prohibitive regulations. In the first few weeks of our imprisonment some of the girls were still pretty despite their shaven heads. Their tattered rags were dirty and so were they, but that didn't seem to bother our tormentors. When the girls were no longer desirable they were sent to the gas chamber. My heart went out to them. After all, what right did I have to condemn those who exchanged sex for food? An extra piece of bread or a cup of "soup" could save them or a loved one from certain death.

These were not the normal circumstances in which prostitution is scorned. There was nothing normal about life in an extermination camp. At home, some young girls went into prostitution for the easy money and carefree living; but in the death camp prostitution meant survival. Hunger is a powerful force that disregards moral codes and ethics.

Yes, life was cheap in the death camp. Hopelessness, helplessness, grief, and torture were a part of our daily lives. The SS guards kicked and savagely beat prisoners for enjoyment. They broke bones and split heads open without even blinking. And anyone could be the next victim.

Two weeks after our arrival in Birkenau, Shari and I, along with thousands of other helpless Jews, were selected for transport to another camp. It was evening when we stood alongside the railroad tracks; our heads were uncovered, and our" dresses," thin and torn, were soaking wet. Many of us, including my sister and I, were without shoes.

The guards taunted us and laughed at our misery. It was easy for them to be jolly for they wore heavy coats, earmuffs, gloves, and scarves. Boots kept their feet warm and fur caps kept the rain off their heads. Every hour they took a break and sat inside the station by a roaring fire. They returned with mugs of steaming hot coffee, which they sipped while they watched us turn blue from the bitter cold.

By the next morning we were even more bitterly cold, but there was still no train. We stood beneath the cloudy sky, dreaming of a cup of hot liquid and a dry, warm corner to rest. At last, well past noon, the rain stopped and a convoy of cattle cars arrived. We were jammed into the dark cars like animals; we huddled together on the bare cold floor trying to keep warm. The wooden planks covering the windows kept the daylight out. We moved again into the darkness of the Nazis' "final solution" to an unknown destination.

Plaszow

I don't know how far or how long we traveled. It may have only been a few hours, but it seemed like an eternity. We were separated from Mother at the end of our earlier journey to Auschwitz, but we prayed that this time Shari and I would be able to stay together.

The train slowed and several prisoners lifted one woman so that she could peek between the boards over the window. We were apparently on the outskirts of a town, she told us, as the train came to a halt and the doors slid open. The camp was in a barren area surrounded by rocky bluffs; it seemed to be in a big hole. It was dusk; another day was about to end and a new chapter behind barbed wire was about to begin.

We hadn't eaten in more than twenty-four hours and we ached with hunger. I felt so dizzy I thought I would collapse, but I managed to follow the others out of the car and into our usual line-up in fives for roll call. Finally, thin slices of bread were passed out, along with a cup of green liquid that barely satisfied our hunger and thirst. I knew I couldn't endure much more suffering and thought death might be near.

It was close to midnight when we put our heads down on the cold, hard floor of the barracks in which dozens of women were squeezed—a place unfit for stabling horses. We hadn't

120

been asleep for an hour when the brutal shouts of the SS guards awakened us. We lined up beneath the starless night for yet another roll call and stood for hours while our guards counted and recounted the thousands of prisoners. We were terrified of what the day had in store for us.

Just before sunrise the guards put us to work carrying rocks that weighed more than we did. We moved the rocks up and down a steep hill and pushed wheelbarrows filled with wet cement and soil. My legs trembled under their weight and my back screamed with pain. For seven weeks we performed this torturous labor by day and stood in endless roll calls at night. The twice-daily ration of a paper-thin slice of bread and the cup of green liquid was far from nourishing. But somehow Shari and I survived.

The lager fuhrer (commandant) of the camp, Amon Goeth, was a vicious sadist. He often participated in the torture and execution of his prisoners. His random killing had nothing to do with the selections that separated those who were near death from those who were still able to work. He shot prisoners merely for sport. The majority of his victims were Jews; others were political prisoners who were also killed in large groups. As we worked on a hill that overlooked the camp, Goeth frequently watched as SS men gunned down prisoners who were lined up against a wall. Some of these victims didn't die instantly and tried to stand. But the guards shot them repeatedly until their bodies were riddled with holes. One day in particular, I saw a large group of prisoners shot to death; and on that same tragic day, a girl who was pushing a wheelbarrow next to me stopped for a few seconds to rest. One of the guards commanded his German shepherd to attack the petrified girl. The dog began tearing off pieces of her famished body and bits of flesh from both of her breasts. The poor girl moaned in whispered tones.

Even death didn't take pity on her as she lay beneath the scorching mid-day sun. Her bewildered, terror-stricken eyes were fixed on the cloudless, blue sky.

We were not allowed to go near her, talk to her, comfort her, or wipe away the tears and sweat from her dying face. The brutal savages were entertained by her unbearable suffering and they kicked the helpless, tormented body. All the while, I thought about my wise grandfather and recalled his last words to us before we were separated. "Believe in God and trust Him. He will always be there to help you." But how was it possible to believe when such monstrous crimes were committed against defenseless, innocent people? I asked God, then, "Where are you?" There was no answer; still, I believed.

Finally, our dear fellow inmate died and we felt great relief knowing that she was at peace.

One morning near the end of August, instead of sending us to work, the guards led us to a waiting line of familiar cattle cars. Rumors of heavy German losses on the eastern front spread around the camp. Our hope was renewed with word that the Allies were approaching, and we also heard that the camp was being closed. The Germans were losing the war, and trying to cover their tracks of mutilation and murder. Auschwitz was again our destination and we knew what that meant.

Return to Auschwitz

We made it through another dark journey. The train stopped and prisoners in blue-striped shirts opened the doors just as they did on our first arrival at Auschwitz. We looked just like them now as we crawled out of the car—human skeletons.

It was difficult to know if was day or night because the sun could not penetrate the smoke that filled the sky. Once again, I saw the tall flames shooting from the crematoria and once again I thought of Mother.

We lined up for roll call knowing that any visible sore, wound, cough, or suspect illness meant death in the gas chamber. Parents and their grown children begged the SS guards to let them go with their loved ones, but they were only ridiculed. The Angel of Death, Dr. Mengele, sent them to their immediate death. Once again, it was our good fortune that Mengele pointed toward life for Shari and me.

We undressed, showered, and were issued clothing that was no better than what we had before; the garments seemed to have more holes than fabric. As we reached the front of the next long line of prisoners, we saw what was ahead of us: much too soon an attendant asked for my left arm. A needle punctured my skin, followed by a thin flow of blood, until the numbers

"17815" were tattooed on my forearm—numbers that replaced my name. That needle went much deeper than the flesh on my arm; it pierced my heart as well. And there it stays forever as a constant reminder that hate and prejudice are the deadliest of diseases and should not be tolerated by the civilized world. We had been branded like cattle and treated like wild animals in the hands of ruthless savages.

The humid, sweltering days were endless. We waited in latrine lines for hours while hordes of insects fed on human waste. I yearned for the privacy of the outhouse that decorated the dusty yard of my home. How I longed to be home with my family and our own private space, the single bed that Shari, my mother, and I shared, and to sit by my grandfather's side listening to his wise words and beautiful stories and feeling his loving touch. I longed for the priceless freedom that I took for granted and lost. Now I had nothing left from my childhood—only the precious memories of my dear father, beloved mother, and wise grandfather, which the passage of time can never erase from my heart.

The prisoners in the A-Lager where Shari and I were placed didn't work; we just waited to die. We had no strength left and sat listlessly on the filthy ground anxiously waiting for our meager meals. At night hundreds of us slept in each barrack, rows of women tightly pressed together on a plank of wood. We could hardly breathe let alone move.

We wore the same torn, colorless, lice-infested rags day and night. Our body lice were more nourished than we were. The parasites that lived on our wretched, emaciated bodies sucked what blood we had left. And diarrhea was as prevalent as the lice, taking a devastating toll on our already weakened bodies. During the night, women crawled over dozens of inmates to go outside to the latrine, but before reaching the door they left trails of loose feces on the floor and on each other.

I would have died from diarrhea and the meager diet if it were not for my brave little sister who managed, on several occasions, to steal some hot cereal from the camp kitchen. But the pounding hunger never ceased and I dreamed about food constantly. It would have been easier to run to the electrified fence and put an end to my misery, but I had to live for Shari.

The gas chambers and crematoria operated twenty-four hours a day, every day; yet they could not handle the enormous numbers of condemned people. Victims waited for death in a holding cell, a barrack adjoining the infirmary. Oftentimes, they were there for three or four days. Mothers with their newborns sat naked, shivering in the damp, cold cells. They kissed their precious babies who were born only to be slaughtered. The tiny newborns clung hungrily to their mothers' milkless, fleshless breasts. Deprived of any nourishment, water, or sleep, the living-dead prayed for a quick end to their misery. Two Jewish nurses, sisters who worked in the infirmary, relieved, temporarily, that misery. These two women managed to steal a few cubes of sugar and diluted those cubes in water, giving a few drops of the sweetened water to each baby. In doing so, the two wonderful nurses sweetened the short and bitter lives of the tiny victims.

When I heard about the sugar cubes, I craved something sweet. I longed for just a crumb, like the crumbs Shari and I looked forward to when my brother was an apprentice confectioner. When we saw Rudi coming home from work in his stained white apron, we ran to meet him and pick at the tiny pieces of cake hidden in the creases of his apron. Like this precious memory, my dreams were consistently about food and home.

125

Sometimes in my dreams, I returned home to Shabbat. It was nightfall and our colorless wooden table was covered with a white cloth and set with chipped, clay dishes. Wildflowers, arranged in a tin cup, adorned the table. A fragile, tiny woman, our beloved mother, stood beside the table. She was dressed in her holiday best, her hair covered with a scarf as she lit the candles to welcome the Shabbat.

The candles flickered in the copper candelabrum, their orange and purple flames the only light in the house. Mother's eyes shone with tears of joy as she embraced us. Grandfather stood beside her, clad in his prayer shawl, his eyes radiating wisdom, his face solemn and serene. He placed his hands on our heads and prayed, and with adoring eyes we looked at him and kissed the hands that blessed us. Outside, the stars were lit as if by angels and glittered like precious diamonds.

Following our simple meal, we sang songs of thanks to the Lord for His generosity. Our house was filled with peace, love, and harmony. We sat in the darkness as the candles melted and extinguished all but the light from the silver moonlight that peeked through the window. Grandfather recited stories from the Bible, and we were bewitched by the magic and supernatural powers of the great prophets and by Grandfather's great wisdom. I wished that my dreams would never end, or if they did end, that I would be home again with my loved ones.

Suddenly, the barking commands of the SS guards brought me back to my horrible reality, and I cried in silence as they ordered us out of the barracks for yet another roll call. My legs were so weak they barely held me up, but I knew I had to be strong to avoid the gas chamber.

One day near the end of September 1944 when we were lined up for roll call, the guards told us that five hundred prisoners would be selected for a transport. When we realized that our friends were not in the chosen group, Shari and I tried to change places with two other women. The SS guards quickly saw the attempt and ordered us back into the line. Fate intercepted, however, for I was the 499th and my sister the 500th inmate to be chosen for the transport.

We followed a row of prisoners toward the cattle cars, and the guards packed us in the cars as tightly as in previous transports. As the familiar clank of wheels on the track began, Shari and I held tightly to each other but spoke not a word. We had survived two weeks in Auschwitz-Birkenau, seven weeks in Plaszow, and another four weeks in Auschwitz. We were afraid to ask and afraid to think where we might be going this time.

Memories of Shabbat

The candle-light glows in the dark
Emitting an amber flame
It is our sacred holy night
Tonight we celebrate.

The silver moon peeks through the window
And greeting us with a smile
Our tiny home shines like a palace
On this divine, Lovely night.

Mother is dressed in her holiday best
Her worries are left behind
Tears of joy are in her eyes
As she's embracing us to her heart.

Grandfather is blessing each of us
And gives us a warm, big hug
We will not go hungry tonight
Tonight, we celebrate Shabbat.

Our home is filled with peace and love
And we feel the presence of God
We thank Him for our simple meal
And for this magical night, Shabbat.

The candles quickly melting away
Our home soon will be dark
But the moonlight is dancing on the walls
And wishing us good night.

Piri Piroska Bodnar

Augsburg

We traveled for days, or so it seemed, not knowing our destination. When our journey finally came to an end, we were surprised to find that we were not at another concentration camp. Instead, we stopped at a train station in Augsburg, Germany, that appeared to have been bombed. The guards pushed us out of the cars, lined us up, and marched us to a row of buildings near the station. There was no barbed wire surrounding this compound which appeared to be some kind of work camp.

We were starved, thirsty, and exhausted when we arrived at Augsburg and couldn't imagine that the building we saw before us would be our living quarters for the next seven or eight months.

Inside one of the buildings were two large halls that had been converted into women's dormitories with bunk beds. They were luxurious compared to the barracks at Auschwitz and Plaszow. Here were wash basins, showers we could use once a week, and flush toilets next door. The facilities didn't accommodate all of the 250 women who slept in each hall, but they were far better than what we had endured so far.

We were lucky to have been selected to go to Augsburg. We heard later that Mariska and all of our cousins and the many friends we left behind in Auschwitz were taken the following day to Bergan-Belsen where they perished.

Augsburg meant life for us, but it was still a life of deprivation and pain. We were locked in the room where we slept, and each morning we were divided into groups and sent to various munitions factories in the area. Armed SS guards led us for miles to one such factory where airplane parts were manufactured. After a little instruction, I was put to work soldering airplane parts. There were no protective devices for our use, and sparks often flew onto my face and into my eyes, burning my eyebrows and eyelashes. It was a miracle that I didn't lose my sight.

It was autumn, the rainy season was upon us, and the leaves were turning to gold, orange, yellow, red, and brown. Our days began before dawn when the stars and moon were still in the black velvet sky. We dragged ourselves to work miles away, with autumn leaves crumbling under our feet. The leaves were dying, and we were dying too, but the golden glow of the German countryside and the smoke curling out of the chimneys of its houses reminded us that life continued despite our plight. We dreamed of being inside one of those houses by a warm fireplace.

The SS guards and their ever-present German shepherds, pushed us to move faster. They kicked us with their heavy boots, beat us with their rifle butts, and lashed our backs with their whips.

The autumn quickly turned into a bitter, cold winter. The pavement was covered with ice and snow. We stumbled and fell; but scraped and bruised, we rose and went on marching. Icicles hung from barren tree branches, and the rooftops were covered with glistening snow. The icy wind blew through our thin, torn rags and through our tired, wasted bodies. Our shaven heads were uncovered and our stockingless feet were bruised, blistered, frostbitten, and bleeding. Each step was taken with excruciating pain.

Other abuse came from local youths who shouted and spat on us as we passed them on the road, using abusive language that had become so painfully familiar. The few people who took pity on us and handed us morsels of food, gave us hope. A potato or a scrap of bread could save a life.

Finally, the long, miserable winter passed and once again nature was coming to life. Tiny buds appeared on the tree branches, and fields were turning green. With the arrival of spring, new hope arose in our hearts. Our sense of hope was also renewed with rumors that the Allies were approaching the city. We knew this was true because the factory building violently shook as their bombs fell all around us.

In the middle of this hope, I suffered a terrible case of eczema. My hand was so swollen and filled with pus that I could hardly bend my fingers, but I still had to work. My main concern, however, was Shari who became seriously ill in early March. At first, she felt exhausted, but then she became very weak and feverish. I held her tiny hot hands and looked into her flushed face; yet it was she who comforted me.

"Piri, the bombing is coming more frequently. The Germans must be worried. The Allies will be coming soon. We can hold on, I know we can," she said.

The following morning a guard unlocked the door and ordered us out of the building and to the waiting cattle cars. As we marched through the town, which had been flattened by bombs, rumors moved quickly among the prisoners that the German command bunker had been destroyed and everyone had been killed. We were being transferred to Dachau, they said.

__Muhldorf__

The hours seemed like days in those overcrowded cattle cars. We stopped first at Dachau, but the camp was so crowded they wouldn't let us in—a fortunate occurrence since tens of thousands had died there by the end of the war. Instead, we were taken to one of the Muhldorf group labor camps under Dachau's administration.

By the time we arrived, Shari's wasted body shook with violent coughing. She was extremely weak, but her will to live was strong. I was devastated, for it was difficult for me to see my sister deteriorate, and I couldn't hold back my tears; yet, it was Shari who kissed them away. "Dear God, I prayed, "please don't let Shari die. I can't live without her. She is the only reason I want to survive." (At that time I had no idea that my brother, Rudi, was alive.)

Shari was so ill that she was unable to work and was placed in a barrack with other gravely ill prisoners. The group I was with worked in a field digging potatoes and turnips. At first I was excited that there might be an opportunity to get food, but we were warned that the penalty for stealing, even a rotten potato skin, was death. While I worked in the fields my heart was with Shari. When I could I brought her whatever scraps I could steal. I was able to do this only when one particular SS officer was on duty. He was a kind human being. He would often watch prisoners steal food and had knowledge that potatoes or turnips were hidden under garments, but he looked the other way.

During the last week of April, American planes flew over Muhldorf dropping bombs on the city and surrounding areas. We were working in the field watching with joy as the bombs exploded around us changing daylight into pitch darkness. It was evident that the end of the war was at hand. Inmates who worked outside the camp told us that the Allies were conquering cities, towns and villages. But the Nazis were determined to finish up their genocide.

One morning following the news, the gravely ill and dying prisoners were lined up in the square where a dozen trucks were waiting. I knew if Shari was loaded onto a truck, I would never see her again. So I sneaked into the line, stood behind my sister, and held her feverish hand.

"I will never let anyone take you from me. We are together and whatever happens we will stay together," I told Shari.

The condemned were loaded into the truck and we knew our turn would be soon. Suddenly, a voice over the loud speaker ordered everyone to return to the barracks. Allied planes were flying over the camp dropping bombs. When the bombing stopped, the SS guards began emptying all the barracks. They nervously watched the sky as they marched all of us out of the camp in rows and loaded us onto the waiting cattle cars. They told us this was our final journey; we were to be executed in a pine forest near Mittenwald.

<u>Liberation</u>

The guards jammed thousands of us into a convoy of boxcars, so closely pressed together that we were hardly able to breathe. After a few hours the train stopped. We held feeble hopes that our guards might give us food or water, but when they opened the doors the unexpected happened. They said we were free to leave. I saw a beautiful green meadow outside the car but I was skeptical about the announcement. I knew too well the dirty tricks the Nazis played.

Many of our fellow prisoners were already dead, but the thought of freedom gave others the adrenaline to get out and run away. Shari and I were so weak, however, that we remained in the car. Nevertheless, the scent of freedom was in the air, so we dragged ourselves from the car.

The meadow was sprinkled with wildflowers and the sun was shining brightly in the blue sky. Many prisoners were already in the meadow and heading toward nearby farms. Our freedom, however, was short-lived. We had barely taken a few steps when we heard machine guns and barking SS commands ordering us back into the train.

The beautiful meadow resounded with the echoes of screaming men and women and was quickly soaked with the sacred blood of innocent victims. Wounded prisoners continued crawling toward the farmhouses on their hands, knees, and stomachs; but they were gunned down before their dreams were fulfilled. Grief-stricken family members knelt beside their loved ones, kissing and stroking their bloody faces and bullet-ridden bodies, but they too were killed. The machine-gun fire didn't stop until nearly everyone in the meadow was dead. The golden sun still shone in the cloudless blue sky, its brilliant rays caressing the ashen faces of the victims; but what right had the sun to shine when in our sorrowful hearts the frost of winter prevailed?

As I dragged myself back toward the cattle wagon amid the dead and dying, I asked myself over and over: "Where is the loving and compassionate God? We need Him so desperately and yet He has abandoned us." I often heard that there is a reason for everything in life, but now that notion was absurd: what was the reason, the purpose, of that bloody massacre and the slaughter of millions at the hands of the Nazis?

We climbed back into the cattle wagons knowing that our own slaughter would take place soon. Shari and I huddled in an embrace, weeping quietly as the death train moved toward its destination.

It seemed like an eternity, but it was only a few hours before the train stopped once again. When the doors were pulled open, we expected to see our SS guards with their machine guns ready to murder those of us who were still alive. But the SS guards had disappeared. The soldiers who opened the doors wore different uniforms and spoke a language different from the Germans. We quickly realized that our prayers had been answered: these were our liberators, the blessed American soldiers.

They embraced us and began to cry. I felt their compassion and love as they looked at us with horror and disbelief. We were human skeletons, barefoot, clad in dirty, tattered rags that barely hung from our ravaged bodies. The soldiers gave us whatever food they had, mainly chocolate and candies, and we couldn't get enough of those delicacies. Unfortunately, many emaciated souls could not digest the rich food, and died.

The majority of our comrades were dead or dying around us. They were placed side by side on the lush green hillside near the town of Tutsing, Bavaria. These were young men, women and teenagers cut down in the prime of their lives. Tears stained their dying, wax-like faces, their eyes open to the clear, blue sky. Our hearts were heavy with pain and sorrow as we said goodbye to our brothers and sisters who died on that glorious liberation day, a day they had yearned for and dreamed about for so long. They were buried in a mass grave—together in suffering, together in eternal peace. May 1, 1945, was a day I will never forget.

In April 1994, almost fifty years later, I learned that, as a prisoner, I was not the only one who would never forget that liberation day. I shared my story at "Yom Hashoah: A Day of Remembrance," an event arranged by students in Dr. Marsha Markman's Holocaust course at California Lutheran University.

As I related the details of that liberation day, a gentleman in the audience stood and introduced himself as Joel Edwards, a ceramicist who taught in the University's Art Department. He asked me to repeat the location where I had been liberated. When I said, "Tutsing," he began to cry.

"I liberated you," he said "I was among those American soldiers who opened the cattle car doors."

I went to him and we embraced and cried, as did many of the spectators in the audience. Words weren't enough for the thanks I owed this man who, almost fifty years before, on the other side of the world, was one of my liberators. And here, in the City of Thousand Oaks, on Holocaust Remembrance Day, of the many survivors whose lectures he might have attended, he chose my session. It was truly a miracle!

Later, Joel shared his moving story with me: He had been part of an intelligence unit that had been moving through the area behind American troops after the Allied bombing. He had heard about the horrors at the camps that had been liberated, but hadn't been prepared for what he saw when he and several other soldiers decided to investigate what appeared to be two abandoned trains.

He said there were two boxcars on one train and three on the other. It seemed strange to see the convoy sitting there in the middle of the countryside. When he and his fellow soldiers opened the door, a packed cattle car of emaciated human beings fell to the ground. Those who were not dead were close to death. He and his comrades tried to tell us they were Americans, but we were frightened and those who could, began running away. We eventually realized we were safe. Joel was so shocked by the sight of human agony, he said, that he shared his experience with only a few people over the years, thinking that nobody would believe him.

Joel came to the Day of Remembrance wanting to hear a survivor's testimony, still trying to believe that what he saw that day in 1945 was not his imagination.

I assured him that he wasn't imagining that dreadful sight because I was one of the prisoners he saw, one who cheated death.

PIRI AND ZOLI

Recovery and Renewal

I had dreamed of liberation for so long that when the day came in 1945, I wondered whether it was only another beautiful dream. The soldiers loaded us in trucks and took us to a displaced persons (D.P.) camp in the nearby town of Feldafing, a former Hitler Jugend (Hitler Youth) camp that had been dedicated to the youth of Hitler's Third Reich. But instead of housing the future hope of Germany, these buildings were now lodgings for the very people Hitler had tried to wipe out.

Right after our arrival at the D.P. camp, we were taken into a large building with a dozen bathtubs. My sister, Shari, and I, along with a few other girls, shared one bathtub, but we didn't care. Our dirty bodies quickly turned the water into mud, but at last we were clean.

After the bath, the American soldiers sprayed us with a disinfectant powder to kill the lice that had infested us during our imprisonment. It felt heavenly to be clean and to wear clean clothes again. The soldiers then escorted us to a huge hall where an elaborate feast was waiting for us. We couldn't eat enough of the ham, cheeses, breads, and chocolates that were so lovingly given to us; how wonderful it was to be treated like human beings again. But we were dehydrated and starved from the long lack of water and nourishment in the camps and couldn't tolerate the rich, fatty foods. Hundreds of people who were liberated across occupied Europe died in the first few weeks after liberation. Fortunately, the medical authorities soon understood the problem and changed the diets.

The soldiers escorted us to a large building that would be our quarters: warm, spacious, well-lit, and well-ventilated rooms. We each slept in a comfortable bed with clean white sheets, a fresh blanket, and a pillow. In addition, we were issued coupons for meals that were served in a large dining hall.

I was well taken care of, yet I didn't feel at ease. Everywhere and everything reminded me of the horror and brutality of the Nazis. My dreams were filled with nightmares about the gas chambers, crematoria, savage beatings and starvation. I wanted desperately to escape from the horrifying memories, but I knew I never could.

The D.P. camp was in Bavaria, not far from Munich and was surrounded by a dense pine forest. However, we couldn't enjoy the beautiful scenery for some time. SS guards and officers hid in the forest and the nights echoed with gunshots. Everyone was fearful that the Nazis would capture us again, and for weeks we lived in constant fear. But our guardian angels, the American soldiers, made sure that no harm came to us.

We all missed our families terribly; and as soon as survivors regained their strength they began to travel to other camps looking for their relatives. Word was passed along about who was looking for whom. Sadly, many of them found that they were the only family members who had survived. Consequently, there was a great need to form relationships and create new families. In the midst of sorrow, life had to continue. Soon, there were concerts, dances, soccer games, and movies. Friendships developed and wedding bells rang.

For a short while Shari and I were together, but she was still so ill with what was diagnosed as tuberculosis that she was taken to a nearby sanatorium. I visited her frequently, and in the meantime kept busy making new friends. One of my friends was a Polish boy named Munyek. He wanted me to marry him and to immigrate to Israel. I liked him, but wasn't in love with him and I didn't want to leave my sister behind. A Greek boy, Peep, also wanted to marry me but I didn't love him either. It was a confusing time. I wasn't sure when "like" became "love" but thought I would know when the right man came along.

And so it happened in late June that a handsome young man who had been liberated from Dachau came to Feldafing. Someone had told him that there were survivors from Miskolc in our camp. Although he had been born in Szendro he worked in Miskolc and knew many people there. I remembered him the moment I saw him. He was my brother Rudi's friend, Zoltan Bodnar. I didn't know him well, but I was flattered that he remembered me.

Zoli, as he was called, was a handsome twenty-year-old man with wavy black hair, large blue eyes, olive skin, and gleaming white teeth. He had a radiant smile and a warm, friendly personality. All the girls at home had crushes on him, but he had a girlfriend then, and I had been just Rudi's younger sister—he never noticed me. That was then, before the war, before the camps, before the Nazis. Now we lived in a different world.

Zoli told me that, like my brother, he had been in a Hungarian labor camp before the German occupation. He and his younger brother had been sent to Dachau seven months before the end of the war. Zoli had arrived with 240 other Hungarian Jews from the labor camps, and only 18 men from his group of 240 had survived. He told me that SS guards beat his fifteen-year-old brother to death.

Zoli decided to stay in our camp, and we spent most of our time together. Those who had trades began earning money and extra food rations. Zoli was fortunate enough to begin working as a barber.

Sometimes we walked to the nearby town of Tutsing. By then I was comfortable enough to walk in the meadow and enjoy the beauty of the Bavarian forest through which we passed. It helped to have Zoli there as my protector. What a joy it was to be free and to wander through the town.

We were in the D.P. camp for five months when Zoli decided to return to Hungary. He felt certain that his parents had survived; they were young and healthy when he saw them last. Therefore, he returned to Hungary to find them. We had no strong commitment to each other, and there was the possibility that Zoli might find his old girlfriend and never come back to me. I was too happy with my freedom to wait and worry while he was gone, so I continued to make new friends while Zoli was away. I met a young, handsome Czech man named Dodo who played the piano beautifully. I didn't fall in love with him, but I fell in love with his music.

However, Zoli remained in my mind and in my heart. When he returned from Hungary, I was overwhelmed with happiness, and we resumed our interrupted relationship. It was pure joy to have him once again by my side. We had so much in common: the past, the present, and a future of possibilities. To be together for the rest of our lives would be—and is—a blessing from God. The news about his family, however, was not good. Someone had seen his mother at Auschwitz with a neighbor who had twin two-year-old sons. She carried one child for her friend when she faced Mengele, and because she held the child in her arms, she was sent to the gas chamber. No one asked whether the child was hers. Zoli's grandparents, he discovered, had also died at Auschwitz.

He found out about his father from a Christian neighbor in his town. Zoli's father was born a Catholic and converted to Judaism when he married Zoli's mother. The authorities told him that if he converted back to Catholicism he would be saved. He asked if this would also save his family, but was told it would not, so he refused to convert and was taken to a labor camp on the Russian front. He died on his way home to Hungary when his train was bombed.

Although Zoli found no survivors from his family, he did not return from Hungary alone. He brought a very precious present for me: my brother, Rudi. When I saw Rudi, I cried and couldn't stop crying, but those were tears of happiness. Rudi had been sent to Mauthausen from the labor camp and later transferred to Buchenwald. After he was liberated from Buchenwald, he returned to Miskolc. He visited my employer, Mrs. Layos, and retrieved our precious family photos and my mother's necklace and ring. I told him about Shari, and we went to see her in the sanatorium. We were concerned that the excitement of seeing Rudi would be too much for her, so Zoli went into her room first to prepare her slowly for the surprise. When she saw Rudi, we all began to cry, kissing and hugging each other, never wanting to let go.

Rudi moved into the basement in Block Four, which Zoli shared with four other friends. Several of them had been confectioners in Hungary, and so discovered a way to earn extra money. There was always a crowd at the soccer games, so Zoli contributed some money for supplies and his friends made pastries to sell at the game. They hoped to double their investment, which was the equivalent of five American dollars. They made two large trays of napoleons and about one hundred pastries. But when they got to the game they were too shy to sell them. They just set them out and waited for people to purchase them. They only sold three pastries.

A friendly Greek man named Bomba wasn't shy about walking through the crowd selling the pastries, and sold all of the napoleons. They broke even on their big business venture and we ate whatever profit there might have been.

Block Four was next to the bathhouse, but there was no water in Rudi and Zoli's room, so Zoli brought water from the bathhouse when I came to do the laundry. On one occasion Zoli was getting hot water without permission and the caretaker locked him in the bathhouse and went for the police. Zoli broke the window and got out of the building, but the camp police came, arrested him, and put him in jail for stealing the water. It seemed like a silly offense, but I suppose they had to have rules to keep order in a camp with 5,000 people.

The camp policeman didn't think Zoli was Jewish because of his name, so Zoli explained that the women in Block B could identify him. The policeman brought him to our living quarters and asked us girls if we knew him. Of course, we all said we did.

"But how do you know he is Jewish?" the policeman asked.

"Because we've seen it," we all giggled and shouted.

Circumcision was proof of being Jewish then and the policeman took our witness as proof, but Zoli still had to stay in jail for two days. Actually, this jail was no prison. Zoli had a skeleton key and each night he left the jail to see me.

The response of the women around me made me realize how popular Zoli was. Many beautiful girls flirted with him, but I knew how much I loved him and didn't want to lose him. One day as we were walking through a meadow I asked him if he had any plans to marry me. Zoli smiled, told me he loved me and asked me to marry him.

A New Life

Because the closest rabbi was in Munich, we decided to be married there. On August 8, 1946 Rudi, Shari, and a group of our friends accompanied us on the short train ride to the city and we were married by a rabbi. What a wedding couple we made: Zoli borrowed a jacket and trousers, but they were too small for him and he couldn't button the jacket. On his head he wore a yarmalka made from newspaper. Nevertheless, he was a handsome bridegroom.

I wore a wedding gown that I made from a white sheet and Zoli picked wildflowers from the meadow, which I carried on my arms and wore in my hair. I'll never forget that beautiful summer day when I became Mrs. Zoltan Bodnar. There was no music, no speeches, no dinner; but our hearts were filled with love. After the ceremony we returned to the D.P. camp and Zoli and I had a romantic dinner for two: scrambled, powdered eggs.

A few weeks later we took a delayed honeymoon. Because Zoli worked at the camp, he was given a week's vacation in a hotel at Oberammergau in the Bavarian Alps. The hotel grounds were overflowing with colorful flowers and surrounded by green meadows. Zoli had to work as a barber in the hotel during the day, but our evenings were free. We watched the golden sunset on the gleaming snowcapped Alps and danced the nights away to the music that floated from the open window of the elegant ballroom.

Back in the D.P. camp, we had different living quarters than what we had enjoyed while on our honeymoon. Only cardboard separated us from other couples who also shared the same room. There was no privacy, so Zoli decided that he would find a better place for us to live. He searched around the camp and found an unfinished building. It had four walls, a roof and a dirt floor, but no doors, windows or electricity. Zoli decided he would make one corner of the building into a little nest for us.

"How can you finish it without building materials?" I asked. Zoli usually received extra rations for his work as a barber and sometimes money too, but even if we had money there was nothing available to buy. Zoli promised he would find a way to finish a room for us to call home. He got together with his friends and they scavenged a door, windows and plaster. He hired a German man to do the plastering and before long surplus rubber mats from the camp dining hall became the floor of our tiny one-room home. We furnished the room with an iron bed, a small wooden table and two chairs. I cooked our meals on a furnace we used to heat the room, and we washed in the community bathhouse which was fun in a way that only young lovers can understand.

The D.P. camp became a little town in the year that I was there. There were shoemakers, tailors, bakers, and barbers and a butcher set up a salami factory in the basement of the building where we lived. (The highest-paid worker was the garbage man!) On one occasion the butcher bought a cow a few miles outside of town and needed someone to sneak the cow into the camp. He offered Zoli five loaves of salami and some money to do it. Zoli and a few of his friends brought the cow through the forest; but when they got to the meadow near the camp, the cow wouldn't stop eating. Leslie, Zoli's friend, took the cow's tail and turned it around and around as if he were cranking the starter on a Model T Ford. The two men shouted at the cow and pushed and pulled until, finally, they got the cow to move. The cow was quickly butchered and sold on the black market, since beef wasn't available legally. Indeed, there was a black market for just about everything, with coffee and cigarettes the most popular currency.

From the basement, the aroma of sausages and salami, prepared with a generous amount of garlic, activated our salivary glands day and night. Well-fed rats lived in the cellar and I'm sure one or two occasionally fell into the grinder to become cold cuts. But, we weren't finicky, and we enjoyed the delicacies that were given to us by the factory owner. During the day the rats came out to sunbathe and settle on our windowsill. They were ugly, vicious monsters and I was petrified of them, but they were not afraid of me. Eventually I had to accept the fact that they were co-owners of our little house.

The sanatorium where Shari was still under medical care was close to the camp. Once she was well enough she visited and frequently spent the night with us. One night she had to go to the outhouse but was terrified of the rats.

"What else can you do, Shari? If you won't go to the outhouse, you'll have to use my hat," Zoli jokingly said. Shari took the offer literally, and taking Zoli's hat, filled it to the brim. When she finished Zoli admitted that it wasn't his hat, but one he had borrowed. We still laugh about it and Zoli has never let Shari forget about that incident.

During the summer, Shari met a handsome young man named Shony who was a survivor of Dachau. He had a passion for music and played the violin exquisitely. Shari and Shony were married and lived near Munich, a short train ride from the camp. The four of us became inseparable. We spent many memorable days together and danced through many nights as Shony played his romantic compositions. Those were precious times; we were young and we were free.

The weeks turned into months and another year passed. We heard that there would be a transport leaving for Sweden in the spring of 1947 and we signed up to go. I had an uncle in Stockholm who offered to let us stay with him until we could get our own place. Uncle Fred was my father's brother, but I had never met him, since he immigrated to Sweden before I was born.

The decision to leave Shari and Shony was painful; but neither Zoli nor I wanted to continue living on the charity of the D.P. camp. Since we didn't want to return to Hungary or remain in Germany, Sweden and Uncle Fred's generous offer seemed a good choice in the next step of our journey together.

Sweden

We left our loved ones and our friends in the D.P. camp in 1947 with a few dollars in our pockets and everything we owned stuffed into a small suitcase. This was to be an adventure with the man I loved. How I wished that my mother had known Zoli, for she would have loved him dearly.

Shari and Shony came to the train station in Munich, where we switched trains for Bergen-Belsen. I stood in the stairwell waving good-bye, not knowing when I would see my loved ones again.

The train took us to the town of Bergen-Belsen home of the notorious death camp where survivors from D.P. camps in the surrounding area were gathered for the trip to Sweden. We were in Bergen-Belsen for two weeks, along with the hundreds of other survivors trying to escape the land of our worst nightmare.

Finally our day of departure arrived. We rode the train to Hamburg, where we spent one night at an inn. The next morning we continued into Denmark—the country that bravely rescued nearly all of its Jews—and traveled on to Copenhagen. The Danish countryside was captivating. We passed picturesque farmhouses with emerald green pastures and country ponds, swans floating among white water lilies. We spent three wonderful days in Copenhagen before boarding the ship to Sweden.

The ship anchored in Landskrona, Sweden where we stayed for ten days while we survivors made plans to settle in different parts of the country. Then we traveled by train to Stockholm, arriving on a clear, star-filled night in 1947. Uncle Fred, a middle-aged, sturdy man, met us at the train station and we took a streetcar to the apartment that he shared with his Swedish girlfriend, Karen, who had a hot meal waiting for us. Although I had never met my uncle before our visit to Sweden, he and Karen were gracious enough to help us in every way they could.

Uncle Fred arranged a job for me at the Frankl Fur Factory and, one day following our arrival, I began working. I didn't like my vocation in Sweden any more than I liked it in Hungary. But my employer was a generous and appreciative man and my coworkers' reassuring smiles and cheerful attitudes made me feel at ease. (Zoli wasn't as lucky. It took him five weeks to find employment at Gustafson's Barber and Hair Styling Salon.) What I remember most clearly about my job was the traditional Swedish coffee breaks. Every day, in mid-morning and mid-afternoon, we enjoyed steaming, strong coffee, cakes and pastries—all set out on a long table for us to eat; and we had a feast.

The months were speeding by, and we yearned to have a place of our own, but hadn't saved enough money. I was feeling downhearted because I wanted to make a home for Zoli and thought we had taken advantage of Uncle Fred's hospitality long enough. Luckily, one evening while taking a walk, we overheard two couples behind us speaking Hungarian. We began a conversation with them and they told us they had been in Sweden only a few months. Otto and Janesi were brothers.

They ran a furrier business from their home with their wives, Margit and Kati. We told them we were looking for a place to live and they told us they had a room for rent.

Their house was filled with laughter one moment and quarreling the next. Every Saturday there was a party, and the aroma of chicken paprikash, Hungarian goulash, and sausages filled the entire apartment building. The guests arrived at six and after filling their stomachs to capacity, the poker games began. It was a loud, smoky, and lively affair that lasted all night. And several times a week all six of us, sometimes even more, squeezed into Janesi's small car and went to the movies.

The lovely summer of 1947 turned into golden autumn, and the withered leaves began to fall. When the winter holiday season arrived, Stockholm looked magical in its kaleidoscope of colored lights and decorations. Every home and store on the street was decorated, and all the trees were covered with ornaments, colorful garlands, and tiny lights.

In the spring of 1948 we left the room we rented from our Hungarian friends and bought the key to our own apartment in Auspuden, a little village on the outskirts of Stockholm. Our apartment building was in a pine forest near a small, sapphire-blue lake. It was a tiny place with one bedroom, a kitchenette and bathroom. We called it our little dollhouse. During spring and summer we spent hours in the enchanting forest picking berries, mushrooms and wildflowers. When winter came we stood by our window watching the snowflakes transform the pine forest into a winter wonderland, the trees shaking beneath the weight of the new-fallen snow.

On the weekends we enjoyed our visits to Djurgarden, where we spent the entire day, taking the ferry to an island that had a zoo and an amusement park. It was a colorful place with open-air concerts and dancing. In the park there were cafes, bakeries, and gift shops. Zoli and I loved the fun-filled atmosphere.

We were grateful and happy to be in a country where people treated us with love and respect and helped us to rebuild our shattered lives. What a great joy it was to be part of a nation where hate and prejudice were absent and where we were not judged by race, religion, or nationality, rather by our virtues.

In 1949 my brother, Rudi, came to Sweden, and I was overwhelmed with joy and excitement. He met a Hungarian woman who was also a Holocaust survivor and they married and lived in a nearby village. Meanwhile, I corresponded with Shari and Shony regularly. One day, they wrote us about their plans to go to the United States, and they asked us to join them. Zoli and I loved our little dollhouse in Sweden, but we missed our loved ones. Clearly, we were faced with a difficult decision. Logic told us to remain in Sweden, but our hearts told us to join Shari and Shony. Shari and I had never been separated for so long and we yearned to see each other. Finally, we made the decision: we would go to the United States.

Because of the limited quota for people emigrating from Hungary, we knew we would not be able to enter the United States immediately. Shari and Shony, who preceded us and settled in Cleveland, advised us to first go to Canada. It would be easier to enter the country as Canadian citizens, and in the meantime we could visit each other. In November 1951, following their advice, we boarded the ship, Stavenger Fjords for Canada where Rudi and his wife, Baba, joined us. With heavy hearts we said goodbye to our beloved Sweden.

With the passage across the icy Atlantic, I left the lands of my ancestors, a continent where the Nazis had carried out the most brutal of crimes against humanity; but the shadows of my experience would be with me forever. My bittersweet memories of childhood, the sorrow of the Holocaust, and the fulfillment of sharing my life with Zoli had made me a survivor who faced the challenge of a new life in a new land.

Piri's grandfather, at home before being forced into the ghetto.

From left: Piri's sister, Shari, her brother Rudi, Piri and their mother.

The street where Piri was born, and lived, in Miskolc.

View of the entrance to the main camp of Auschwitz I in Upper Sillesia, Poland where Piri was sent on two occasions. The gate bears the motto, Arbeit Macht Frei (work makes one free). United States Holocaust Memorial Museum, courtesy of Instytut Pamieci Narodowej.

Plaszow concentration camp, Krakow region, Poland, where Piri was forced into slave labor. In the foreground, a group of Jewish women are marched to work.
Courtesy of U.S. Holocaust Memorial Museum Photo Archives, Leopold Page Photographic Collectiion, Instytut Prmieci Narodowej.
Photographer: Raymund Titch, 1943-1944.

Plaszow concentration camp, Krakow region, Poland. Jewish women prisoners, like Piri, are shown in a slave-labor brigade. Courtesy of United States Holocaust Memorial Museum, Photo Archives. Photographer, Raimund Titch, 1943-1944.

Epilogue

From Piri's Notebook

It was a gloomy, miserable day with the temperature at twenty below zero when the *Stavenger Fjords* anchored in the harbor of Halifax, Nova Scotia. There was no one waiting for us, and we felt lonely and homesick for our beloved Sweden. A few hours slipped by before our connecting train to Montreal pulled into the station. The countryside and villages we passed were sleeping beneath a white carpet of snow.

We arrived in Montreal in the middle of a snowstorm; the roads and sidewalks were a solid sheet of ice. We were strangers in a strange city, waiting anxiously in the bitter cold night for the city bus to take us downtown. The room we rented was in an old, neglected apartment building, but the rent was cheap. Luckily, two months following our arrival in Montreal, Zoli found a job and we were able to move. Our apartment on Barclay Avenue was in a nice working-class neighborhood.

I worked for a furrier until our precious baby, Kitty, was born. After her birth, Zoli and I decided that I would stay home and raise our child. To make ends meet we rented out one of our two bedrooms.

Time flew by, and when Kitty was four years old our treasured son, Eric, was born. Kitty adored her baby brother and was protective of him. The love they shared as children continues today. For Zoli and me, our children were the center of our lives, and their welfare and well-being have always been our first priority.

We lived in Montreal for seven years and became Canadian citizens, but our aim was to immigrate to the United States. In 1958 our dream came true when we received our affidavit. With two small children and five hundred dollars, our journey began. We settled in Los Angeles, California where my brother, sister and their families lived. Within a few weeks Zoli received his California barber's license and began to work. We were so very happy. Our apartment on Clemson Street was in a relatively new neighborhood with children Kitty and Eric's ages. Outside, the lawn was well-kept and decorated with flowering shrubs and shady trees. We still have fond memories of our lives there.

In 1963 we became citizens of our dearly beloved country, the United States, and in 1974 we moved out of Los Angeles. Our new home was in a small, quiet, community with sweet, clean air. There was plenty of open space, a lake across from our home, beautiful green fields sprinkled with colorful poppies, larkspur, daisies, and mustard plants. And at night the sky was alive with glittering stars. Agoura was our paradise.

Zoli owned a barbershop in Westlake Village and it was flourishing. Indeed, we were content. Our children were growing into beautiful adults. Kitty, earned a Bachelor of Science degree in Criminal Justice from California State University, Los Angeles, a Master's Degree in Public Administration (MPA) from California Lutheran University, and a law degree (J.D.) from The Southern California Institute of Law, Santa Barbara.

Our son, Eric, attended Moorpark College and, following graduation, continued his studies at California State University, Los Angeles, majoring, as did his sister, in Criminal Justice.

Both Eric and Kitty were excellent students and graduated with honors. Zoli and I are very proud of their academic achievements, but more importantly, they make us happy for they have high morals and are compassionate, caring human beings.

Currently, Kitty is Adjunct Professor in the School of Business and Global Studies at the University of LaVerne. Two key courses that she teaches are: "Business Ethics" and "Gender and Culture Issues in Management." She and her wonderful husband, Don Plank—our second son—have been happily married for thirteen years. Don is also an educator and both he and Kitty love their chosen professions and are adored by their students.

Following graduation, Eric worked for the Los Angeles County Sheriff's Department. His career has brought him numerous awards. The most precious one resulted from an incident that occurred on July 22, 1984 as he was returning home from work. From the freeway he noticed smoke covering the sky and fire leaping from a twelve-story building, a retirement home in Reseda, California. He drove off the freeway and to the scene, identified himself as a Sheriff's Deputy, and offered to help the firemen. Before the fire was extinguished, Eric had carried dozens of fragile people on his back and out of the burning building.

The newspapers reported the event and as a result of Eric's heroism, he received awards from city officials and the Meritorious Conduct Gold Medal from the Sheriff's Department. His rescue efforts didn't surprise us, for we always knew that God blessed us with a special angel.

My sister, Shari, and her family remain close to us and to our children. Shony, who was like a brother to us, became a renowned violinist, recording his works and performing all over the world. Tragically, he died in 2002. His music, however, remains a vital part of our lives. My brother Rudi, too, has died leaving me with beautiful memories of our childhood and our lives together following liberation.

We are in the twilight of our lives now and enjoy each precious moment that we share together and with our family. As we look back upon our lives we realize how very lucky we were to survive the massacre of the Nazi Holocaust. Our paths were bumpy, with many obstacles to overcome. The haunting memories of the Holocaust are engraved forever in our hearts. But we are deeply grateful to God and thank Him every day for the most precious of gifts which He has bestowed upon us: our dear children.

To them, our "Sunshine," Kitty, and our "Guardian Angel," Eric, who bring so much joy into our lives, God bless you.

With All Of My Heart

I treasure the day when you and I met
That splendid lovely spring I never will forget
You brought meaning into my empty life
And lit up my day with your loving smile.

On our wedding day the sun was shining bright
Butterflies were playing on the clear, blue sky
The air was filled with the fragrance of lilies
And birds were singing enchanting melodies

We began to build our tiny loving nest
Life was very hard, but hope and faith we had
We were looking forward to having a family
And knew it would make us completely happy

Together we had raised our precious children
You worked very hard to provide for them
To give them all the things which you never had
Their smiling faces were your greatest happiness

Five decades passed by in happiness and tears
You were always near to erase my pain and fears
And as we approach the twilight of our lives
I thank the Lord and you, for fifty years of love.

Piri Piroska Bodnar

<u>*To My Precious Children*</u>

This poem is my present to you
Each word is speaking of love
How very dear you are to me
With simple words I try to describe

Your smiling face lights up my day
And fills my heart with joy
Your laughter music to my ears
You are my pride, my world

When you are feeling sad or down
My heart is breaking too
I cannot bear to see you cry
Because I love you so

I thank God each single day
For the treasures that I have
Each moment that I spend with you
Truly priceless and precious

I pray to God to give you health
Long life and happiness
And guard over you day and night
And guide your every step.

Piri Piroska Bodnar

Kitty, Piri and Eric, 1960.

Eric receiving a Meritorious Conduct Award, 1985.
From left: Sheriff Sherman Block, Los Angeles County
Sheriff's Department, Piri, Eric, Kitty and Zoli.

Eric's award.

For his heroic action on July 22, 1984, when, while off duty, he observed smoke and flames emitting from a twelve-story retirement home and placed himself in immediate peril by repeatedly entering the structure and safely evacuating more than twenty senior citizens, the Los Angeles County Sheriff's Department presents the Meritorious Conduct Medal – Gold, this twenty-fifth day of January, nineteen hundred and eighty-five, to

Deputy

SHERMAN BLOCK, SHERIFF

From left: Zoli, Kitty, Piri and Eric at Kitty's law school graduation, 1989.

Kitty and husband, Don. Undated photo.

Piri, Zoli, Kitty and Eric at Zoli's 70ᵗʰ birthday party.

Family gathering, 2004. Piri and her sister Shari (front row).

From left: Piri's sister Shari, brother Rudi,
and Piri in California.

Timeline

March 1944   German occupation of Hungary

April 1944   Beginning April 16, the first day of Passover, the concentration of Hungarian Jews into ghettos began. The Mendelovits family moved to the ghetto where they remained for approximately six weeks.

May 1944   Beginning on May 15, Hungarian Jews were deported To Auschwitz. The Jews from Miskolc and the surrounding area were moved to a brick factory outside the city. At the end of May, the Mendelovits family was moved from the ghetto to a brick factory in Diosgyor, about six kilometers from the ghetto. Zoli's mother and grandparents were also taken to the ghetto.

June 1944   From June 11 to June 15 Miskolc's 10,000 Jews were deported to Auschwitz. In mid-June the Mendelovits and Bodnar families were deported to Auschwitz from the brick factory.

At the end of June, after two weeks in Auschwitz, Piri and her sister, Shari, were deported to Plaszow, where they remained for seven weeks. (May and June 1944 saw the greatest number of prisoners at Plaszow: 24,000 including from 6,000 to 8,000 Hungarians.)

In the summer of 1944 the Red Army was drawing near, and work began on breaking up the camp. Prisoners were transferred to other camps.

August 1944   Piri and Shari were returned to Auschwitz, where they remained for four weeks. At the same time, Zoli was quartered in a synagogue in Hejocsaba, a Hungarian labor camp.

September 1944   Piri and Shari were transferred to Augsburg concentration camp (a work camp under the Dachau Concentration camp commander in the Augsburg area. An average of 540 female prisoners worked for the Michelwerke factory near Haunstetten, first mentioned on June 11, 1944 in Dachau records.)

October 1944   Zoli was marched to the German border and then into cattle Wagons enroute to Landsberg labor camp.

November 1944   Zoli arrived in Landsberg, a subcamp of Dachau, where he remained until liberation.

March 1945	Piri and Shari were moved to Muhldorf Concentration Camp in mid-March, where they remained for four-to-six weeks. (The "Muhldorf Group" of Dachau Concentration Camps was located in several villages in the Muhldorf area. Waldalager VI: 250 female prisoners were held at Ampfing, five miles west of the city.)
April 30, 1945	Dachau concentration camp was liberated and Zoli was freed.
May 1945	Piri and Shari were liberated on May 1st while being transported by train to the Mittenwald forest for execution.
August 1946	Piri and Zoli marry.
1947	Piri and Zoli emigrate to Sweden.
1948	Shari emigrates to the United States.
1949	Piri's brother, Rudi, emigrates to Sweden
1951	Piri and Zoli emigrate to Montreal, Canada. Rudi and Baba join them two months later.
1957	Rudi and Baba emigrate to the United States.
1958	Piri and Zoli emigrate to the United States and settle, first in Los Angeles and currently in Agoura Hills, California.

Dana J. Cordero

Sources Consulted

Brahan, R.L., "Jews During the Holocaust." *Encyclopedia of the Holocaust.* Vol. 2. New York, Macmillan Publishing Co., 1990.

Dawidowicz, Lucy S. *The War Against the Jews, 1933-1945.* New York: Bantam Books, 1986.

Roth, John K., and Richard L. Rubenstein. *Approaches to Auschwitz: The Holocaust and Its Legacy.* Atlanta: John Knox Press, 1986.

Rozett, Robert, "Miskolc." *Encyclopedia of the Holocaust.* Vol. 2. Israel Gutman, ed. New York: Macmillan Publishing Co., 1990.

About the Authors

In 1944 Hungary Piri Piroska Mendelovits and Zoltan Bodnar were nineteen years old, each apprenticing to augment their families' income: Zoltan to a barber and Piri to a furrier. When the Nazis invaded Hungary they, along with their fellow Jews, were forced from their homes and into ghettos, slave labor camps, and concentration camps in Poland and Germany. Under that system they endured and witnessed unprecedented brutality in forced labor and in the death camps where they were certain their lives would end. Liberation came at the brink of their very existence.

The pair met in a Displaced Persons Camp in Germany. They fell in love and married in Bavaria near the camp; and like so many young survivors, they were determined to begin life anew and replenish their stolen lives, for in two large families only Piri's sister and brother survived the Holocaust.

Both writers reflect on the joy and pain of liberation, and the journey that led them to a welcoming and renewed life in Sweden. There they lived and worked for several years before immigrating to Canada and finally to the United States to join Piri's sister and brother.

Zoli operated his own barbershop, until he retired in 2004. Piri, also retired, studied and practiced nursing in Los Angeles. She has audited classes at California Lutheran University since 1989 and speaks regularly to students about her Holocaust experiences. Her 1998 memoir, *Shadows*, describes those events. In 2003, she was honored by the University for her contributions as a lecturer, mentor and friend. Both Piri and Zoltan who has joined his wife at several lectures, carry the message of remembrance of the Holocaust and of other acts of hatred and genocide to students in area colleges and universities. They make their home in California near their son Eric, daughter, Kitty and their "second son," their son-in-law, Don.

Printed in the United States
79233LV00008B/79-81